HOW

TRANSCENDENTAL TOYBOX

UPDATE NO. 1:
THE COMPLETE GUIDE TO
2OO3 MERCHANDISE

HOWE'S TRANSCENDENTAL TOYBOX

UPDATE NO. 1:
THE COMPLETE GUIDE TO
2003 MERCHANDISE

BY DAVID J HOWE
& ARNOLD T BLUMBERG

First published in England in 2004 by

Telos Publishing Ltd
61 Elgar Avenue, Tolworth, Surrey, KT5 9JP, England
www.telos.co.uk

in cooperation with

ATB Publishing Inc.
33 Silverton Ct, Cockeysville, MD, 21030
www.atbpublishing.com

Telos Publishing Ltd values feedback. Please e-mail us with any comments you may have about this book to:
feedback@telos.co.uk

ISBN: 1-903889-57-X (paperback)

Internal design, typesetting and layout by Arnold T Blumberg. Page top border collages by Nathan Skreslet.

Printed in India.

1 2 3 4 5 6 7 8 9 10 11 12 13 14 15

British Library Cataloguing in Publication Data.
A catalogue record for this book is available from the British Library.

WE'RE very proud to present the first annual update volume to *Howe's Transcendental Toybox*, covering all of the *Doctor Who*-related merchandise released in the 40th anniversary year, 2003. As with the two full editions of this guide before it, we hope you enjoy this unique voyage through the universe of *Doctor Who* collecting.

In any project of this size and scope, errors are bound to creep in despite our best efforts. If you discover any inaccuracies, or have photos or information that should be included in a future edition, please feel free to contact us directly (our e-mail addresses are listed below). Although we welcome the feedback, please note that we cannot enter into any private communications regarding any aspects of pricing or related collectible topics. While we're interested to know what's out there, we simply can't always respond personally to queries. We hope you'll still feel motivated to write and let us know what you think of our efforts.

In the end, this isn't just our guide to the world of *Doctor Who* merchandise...it's yours too. With the series scheduled for a long-awaited return to UK TV in 2005, this is the perfect time to either explore the fun and fascinating universe of *Who* collectibles once again, or discover it for the very first time. Now where did we put that TARDIS key?

Cheers,
David J Howe (david@telos.co.uk)

Arnold T Blumberg
(the14thdoctor@yahoo.com)

ACKNOWLEDGEMENTS

FOR this 2003 update volume of the TOYBOX, the authors would like to thank the following individuals and organisations for their kind help and support:

Keith Barnfather (Reeltime Pictures), Barrie Roness (Strictly Ink), Steve Walker (Product Enterprises Ltd), Gary Russell (Big Finish), Steve Scott (The Stamp Centre), Lars Pearson (Mad Norwegian), Alan Stevens (Magic Bullet), and Ann Kelly (BBCi).

Thanks also for research assistance to Steve Manfred (for US release information), Tony Keywood (for Australian release information), Stephen James Walker, Roger Smith (at Mr Models), Matthew Fitch, Kevin Anderson, Paul Scoones (for New Zealand release information), Jon Preddle, Steven Smith (pictures), Richard Briggs (pictures), and Anthony Forth.

And a belated special thanks to Martyn Alner, who graciously provided the colour cover scans for the *Doctor Who* Magazine gallery in the second edition of the TOYBOX and who continues to support us with information.

WELCOME to the wonderful world of *Doctor Who* collectibles! If you grew up with the Doctor, joined his adventures later in television repeats or on video and other media, or if you're an SF-TV enthusiast who likes to learn more about the history of science fiction fandom and collectibles, then you've come to the right place.

This book is an add-on volume to the second edition, which documents the entire range of *Doctor Who* merchandise produced and released since the show started on BBC television on the 23rd November 1963, up to the end of 2002. Here we primarily look at the items released in 2003 – the year of *Doctor Who*'s 40th anniversary – and discover the incredible array of items released in just one year! All of the items are listed by category, and for the most part, all the information in this book has been researched through first-hand viewing of the items concerned, while other information has been gleaned from other sources.

We've tried to make the listings as easy to follow as possible. Each item is listed by an item code (assigned by us in relation to the category in which the item is listed, and which continues the numbering sequences from the main edition) and its name. In some cases this is the actual name given by the producers of the items, while in other cases we've named an item with an approximate description that best identifies the collectible in question. Because of the sheer quantity of items included, there will be occasions when readers may find it difficult to locate an item as it may not be listed where perhaps it might be expected. Please try alternative locations in these instances: for example a book you expected to find under 'Books, Factual' might be under the 'Books, General' heading, or an 'Activity Book' might be under 'Books, Gaming'. We have tried to apply common sense to the

locating of items, and we hope that this sort of confusion will not often happen.

We also list release dates (as accurate as we have been able to determine; sometimes this is just the year, sometimes a year and month, and occasionally the actual date of release) along with any other pertinent descriptive information (manufacturer, distributor, size, colour etc.). A reference number is sometimes listed (a serial number or ISBN code), as well as the original retail price when known. Finally, a current Near Mint value is listed when it could be reasonably determined (see our notes on pricing later in this article). Prices are generally given in UK pounds sterling as the UK is where the majority of items are produced for sale, and where Near Mint pricing tends to be more consistent. For the 2003 items, these are generally too new for there to be a Near Mint value of any significant difference to the original retail price.

CRITERIA

THIS section explains the scope of the *Toybox* project, and is meant to help readers understand our criteria for including items.

First of all, we decided that we could not include anything and everything which could be classed as a *Doctor Who* collectible; there is far too much. Therefore we developed a basic inclusion criterion: items had to have been available to buy commercially, and also needed to be *Doctor Who* items in their own right. Collectible items like autographs, props, costumes, scripts and other production documentation, photographs (except where commercially available), proof copies and other manufacturing trial items are therefore not included as they do not fall into this definition.

There are, of course, some instances where we broke our own rules. The main exception are the comic strips which appeared in places other than *Doctor Who Magazine* (and its variant titles) and a 2003 appendix of these appears at the back of the book. We have not listed magazine articles, newspaper articles or any other *Doctor Who* coverage in the press with the exception of particularly relevant editions of the BBC's listings magazine *Radio Times* (those with *Doctor Who* covers in particular).

We have also generally excluded items produced by fans and fan clubs except where these were commercially available. Fanzines and fan magazines have not been included. Occasionally, however, we have allowed some fan-produced items to creep in, particularly where they were of note or of professional quality.

We have not generally included promotional items and point of sale items. For items to be included, they must have been generally available to buy.

There are some other basic notes on the inclusion of items, and the content of the text, which are worth mentioning:

To keep the list as concise as possible, we assume that the reader has a basic knowledge of *Doctor Who* and the various people involved in its creation and realisation. Notes are sometimes provided as to the backgrounds of several individuals involved in the creation of the merchandise, but these are not all-inclusive, and the intention is not to provide biographical information on the show or its production. For anyone who wants to know more about *Doctor Who* generally, we'd recommend the Telos edition of *The Television Companion* (by David J Howe and Stephen James Walker), available from Telos (www.telos.co.uk) and other retailers, as a good starting point.

We also only list those items which were actually released. There is a listing of some announced but unreleased items for 2003 – or 'ghost' items as they have been termed – at the back of the book in Appendix B.

Information has been supplied where known. If a description or information is absent, it means that it is not known. We have tried not to assume things in the listings.

We have tried to keep the information factual, and avoided passing opinion on the items except where this forms a part of the background or is relevant to the collectibility or desirability of an item.

Where a product features foil printing, the chances of there being mis-prints with the foil either missing or mis-aligned are quite high. Plastic toys can also be found in variant colours from those they were 'officially' released in. These variants are collectible, but are not necessarily worth a great deal more than their 'standard' counterparts.

ABBREVIATIONS

THROUGHOUT this series of books we employ a variety of abbreviations and acronyms to refer to common terms, company names, and other information that regularly applies to *Doctor Who* merchandise. Here are some of the most frequently used abbreviations:

TARDIS – The Doctor's time capsule, disguised to look like a British police telephone box. The letters in TARDIS stand for Time And Relative Dimension in Space.

b&w – Black and white

BBC – The British Broadcasting Corporation, the television home of the Doctor.

c. – circa. Where actual dates cannot be determined, we've used this to indicate uncertain dating.

CBS/FOX – At one time, the United States distributor of *Doctor Who* on video.

Audio

C – Cassette

CD – Compact Disk

DVD – Digital Versatile Disk

LP – Long Playing Record

EP – Extended Playing Record

7" – Seven inch single

12" – Twelve inch single

Books

h/b – Hardback.

p/b – Paperback. Either a standard 'A' format paperback or a slightly larger 'B' format version.

lfp/b – Large Format Paperback. A large softcover edition.

l/b – Leatherbound.

ISBN – International Standard Book Number. All published books should have an ISBN allocated to them.

ISSN – Like the book numbering system, but used for magazines and periodicals.

SBN – Standard Book Number. Sometimes used rather than ISBN.

Clothing

S – small

M – medium

L – large

XL – extra large

CONDITION

ETERMINING the condition and relevant grade of an item for purposes of pricing in the collectible market is probably one of the most contentious areas of discussion in collectibles today. Philosophical wars are fought in the unlikeliest situations merely to establish whether a book is considered in Fine condition or Near Mint. We advise all those interested in collecting to base the evaluation of an item's condition on the easily identifiable physical factors listed below. Beyond that, we would suggest that when looking to purchase an item, your own desire to own the collectible and your opinion of its condition is all that matters in the end. The choice to buy or not to buy is always yours, and if you're unhappy with the condition of a collectible, whether it's marked as Good or Mint, the power to walk away is always yours as well.

For the newcomer to collecting and the seasoned convention goer alike, we've assembled here a basic list of grading terms and their definitions. Please remember that these are loosely defined areas for purposes of evaluation, and the grade and condition of an item is ultimately a subjective determination made by the seller and the buyer.

The physical condition of an item is probably the primary means of evaluating its value in the marketplace, if only because it relies purely on visual indicators. Other factors in determining value, like rarity and demand, are more esoteric, and require a bit more research. For the most part, although these grades are subjective, the terms and their application will be familiar to most of the collectible community. At the very least, you will be armed with a common language that will allow you to buy and sell in an informed way.

One last note: since almost all collectibles have been handled at one time or another, it is almost impossible to find any item that can be considered to be in Mint (i.e. "perfect" or original) condition. Therefore we begin our grading range with the term Near Mint, indicating an item that is nearly new in every way apart from the most minor wear. This is the standard upon which we have chosen to base the pricing for this book. Anything less than this, therefore, should theoretically cost less than the prices herein. Variations on this grading scale are used by collectors worldwide in relation to items like comic books, toys, and other ephemera, and serve as a useful 'universal language' in the collectible community.

In general, most collectors follow a grading system that employs the grades of Mint, Near Mint, Very Fine, Fine, Very Good, Good, Fair and Poor. There are distinct variations in the nomenclature and the ways in which these grades are practically applied to each hobby, but the basic meanings remain the same. Some specific notes on the application of these grades:

NEAR MINT–The highest grade that can be expected in most collectible categories. Paper items are still bright with little visible wear, lay flat, and if there are any staples they are rust-free. Metal or metallic items retain their lustre and any applied colouring. There is no corrosion or rust, and any working parts (or pins in the case of badges) must still operate. In the case of celluloid badges (those that have a plastic coating to seal in photographic or graphic material), the items must be free of stain or discoloration. There can be no surface scratches or splits.

FINE–Paper items display moderate wear and ageing, including creases and small tears, worn corners, a small amount of browning or yellowing, light rust around staples, and other assorted minor defects. Metal objects still retain about 50-60% of their original lustre. Corrosion or rust may be evident in small amounts, and moving parts may be slightly bent or damaged. Other materials may show scratches, minor dents, discoloration, chipping, and other stress markings.

GOOD–Paper items must still be intact, with no more than a few small pieces missing. Obvious ageing, creases, tears, browning, and other defects are evident but the item is more or less complete. Metal objects have lost almost all lustre and possible applied colouring, with repaired or

lost working parts. Other major defects and surface stress are evident, but again the items must be complete. Other materials can exhibit ageing, discoloration, staining, stress fractures, and other obvious wear. Key to retaining this grade is that items must not display so much wear as to make them totally undesirable for collectors.

Again, keep in mind that these are only meant to be general guidelines, and as such they are subject to interpretation depending on the item in question and the collector's desire to obtain it. We have chosen to reflect values that adhere to the upper end of this scale for brevity and practicality.

DETERMINING VALUE

IF there's anything in the world of collectible price guides more contentious than grading condition, it's the actual pricing of individual items. There's no doubt that once again, this must be based at least in part on subjective evaluation, but the credibility of a guide like this must stand or fall on the accuracy, and more importantly, the honesty, of its pricing data.

As most die-hard collectors will tell you, pricing is a tricky thing, based on factors such as condition, demand for the item in question, and its rarity in the marketplace. Is this a common collectible, produced in the hundreds of thousands or millions for distribution to stores? Was this a limited edition release, difficult to find in good condition today? Was this a promotional item, perhaps only available to those connected to someone in the industry and thus an extremely rare item of considerable value?

For the most part, it can be easily determined how rare an item is by finding out how many were made and how many still exist. If, for example, only three intact copies of a certain comic book exist, then it's naturally quite rare. If it was a 1980s issue printed in the millions, it's pretty common. Either way, the rarity of an item is ultimately quantifiable. This is not, however, always true. For example, print runs are known for the majority of the first edition Target novelisations; however, a handful are considerably harder to find than the majority, despite their print runs being of similar magnitude. Manufacturers tend to guard their sales figures rigorously and it can be hard to find out the information. Where known, we have included print run and unit sale information in the listings.

It's an entirely different matter when dealing with demand and condition. Since we've already discussed grading, we must take a moment to examine the concept of demand in collectibles. A book like this is probably already reaching an audience at least mildly if not wildly interested in the subject matter. Therefore, all of the items listed here are in demand to some extent as *Doctor Who* collectors scour the market for treasured items from the past. Some items, however, may enjoy more appeal and demand due to their subject matter. A Tom Baker toy or magazine is arguably more recognizable and more desirable than say, a Colin Baker or William Hartnell item. On the other hand, collectors devoted to the series who grew up watching different Doctors may focus their efforts on those eras in the show's merchandise history, and for them, a Hartnell or Troughton item may be the most important find of all.

Ultimately, as noted before in matters of grading, a collectible is worth what you think it's worth. Everyone has their own opinion as to how important a collectible is, what minimum condition it must be in to commit to the sale, and how much they're willing to spend. For collectors, the collectible market is not about pounds and pennies or dollars and cents...it's about the heart and cherished memories. There's no way to put a value on nostalgia, but if both the buyer and the seller can agree on terms, then everyone can be happy. There are a few other factors important in determining the value of an item. Certainly in the case of *Doctor Who*, there is the potential for cross-over appeal. *Doctor Who* fans will naturally be interested in collectibles related to the show, but so might general SF fans, as well as fans of cult television or British pop culture history, for example. Even collectors of robots will want to have the Dalek toys in their possession, and someone interested in obscure plates could be hunting the 1999 *Day of the Daleks* item. If diverse groups of collectors are interested in an item, the chances are it enjoys a higher profile in the market, and subsequently a higher value.

Another significant factor in play where *Doctor Who* is concerned is geography. For collectors on either side of the Atlantic, finding that sought after item may be difficult if the country of origin and its likeliest resting place is miles away. United States fans eager to own *Doctor Who* collectibles may pay much more for UK items that rarely turn up in the States, while UK fans may be willing to value a US or Australian item a bit higher than one they can easily find at the local comic shop.

All of these elements must come into play when determining the value of an item. But even so, it's far more difficult to consider all of these factors in order to print a definitive value in a guide rather than just come to terms between buyer and seller at a convention or in a store. So how did we establish the prices in this book without weighing one factor too heavily or allowing too much bias to enter into the process?

VALUES LISTED

MOST successful, reliable guides today realise that valuing the items listed in their pages involves traversing the most dangerous territory any guide publisher can hope to navigate. In order to guarantee that the values listed are as accurate and as balanced as possible, these guides employ a number of advisors chosen from the collectible community and recognized as experts in their field. These advisors, typically a cross-section of retailers, dealers, professional collectors and pop culture historians, provide notes and detailed pricing information based on actual sales tabulated during the course of the last year to establish the values for the market in question.

In the case of this series of books, we initially contacted and enlisted the aid of many other experts, dealers and collectors, most of whom are listed in the acknowledgments page at the beginning of the second volume. Their opinions and documented data were invaluable in setting the prices published there. For this edition, as stated above, generally Near Mint prices are not given, but one or two items have already sold out, and are now fetching higher prices in the secondary marketplace. Any such prices should be taken as for 'Near Mint'. In other words, these are guide prices for an item which is complete, boxed and totally undamaged and unmarked. Any other condition, and you should expect the prices to be lower. Pricing is an imprecise art, and the value of any item is really what the buyer is prepared to pay. Therefore please take all valuations in this book as a guide only, and the authors take no responsibility for actual pricings or prices paid by collectors.

We tended to not include any values taken from auctions as these vary wildly and are not an accurate representation of the true worth of an item. While it is true that Internet-based auctions have become an intrinsic part of the experience for many pop culture collectors, it remains a difficult task to ascertain the value of an item based on that kind of sales activity. The major Internet auction site eBay, for example, has played a significant role in setting unheard-of records for high prices paid in the comic book collecting community, but the prices realised in an eBay auction usually diverge drastically from prices realised in a traditional convention or retail environment. Is this the way collectibles pricing will be determined from now on, or is this merely one way of looking at the market? For our purposes, eBay and other Internet auction activity did inform some of our thinking, but did not wholly dictate our final decision on the values contained in this range of books.

We cannot stress enough, however, that these prices are merely guidelines. We are suggesting values, not dictating them. Furthermore prices can rise or fall depending on availability and demand. The decision about whether or not an item is worth a certain amount must be the determination of the individual buyer or seller, and the true value of a collectible is however much you as a collector are willing to pay for it. The most important thing is to have fun and enjoy the thrill of collecting.

2003 OVERVIEW

BY DAVID J HOWE

"One of the BBC's best-loved cult sci-fi programmes last seen on British TV in 1989, *Doctor Who* celebrates its 40th Anniversary in November 2003. There continues to be a huge market for *Doctor Who*-related products and merchandise; already during the anniversary year, BBC Video and DVD total sales passed the three million mark. BBC Audio Books has sold more than 250,000 audios across 42 titles and BBC Books will have published over 100 original *Doctor Who* novels making the series the largest ever book range built around a single principal character. To commemorate *Doctor Who*'s 40th anniversary, BBC Worldwide has developed an anniversary logo for use on all related merchandise along with a style guide. BBC Worldwide is looking to work with licensees to develop a range of *Doctor Who* merchandise to complement the comprehensive range of published products in audio, book, video/DVD, magazine, music and internet form launching throughout 2003 and beyond."

BBC Worldwide Press Release, 2003

One year. One anniversary.

There had been many who had felt that the 25th anniversary would be the last that *Doctor Who* fans would celebrate...and then people had said that there was no life past the 30th, and then that the 35th was the final time we'd get to party. But 40 years on, *Doctor Who* shows no sign of slowing down.

In 2003 alone, there were around 200 individual items of merchandise released world wide – more than twice as many as the 100-odd Dalek-related items released at the height of Dalekmania in 1964 and 1965. By far the biggest producers of *Doctor Who*-related items in 2003 were BBC Worldwide themselves, and Big Finish. BBC Worldwide released

approximately 34 items across all their ranges of books, DVDs, videos and audios, and Big Finish accounted for around 36 items, mostly in their range of original cast CD dramas, but also in short story collections and script books.

It's not surprising that BBC Worldwide would want to keep a close eye on one of their most well-loved and profitable franchises for the 40th anniversary year, but some of their decisions in the run-up to that period seemed somewhat hard to fathom to independent observers. Sometime during the course of 2002, they decided to make *Doctor Who* the focus of a rebranding exercise, and recruited new staff into their Licensing division to handle this. Then they started to review all the existing licences, and made a decision to cut back on those that they felt were not in keeping with the new direction in which they wished to take the *Doctor Who* brand. Speaking to *Doctor Who* Magazine in April 2003, Siobhan Williamson, one of the Licensing Managers, explained that they were looking to 'broaden [their] market', and asserted that the best way to do that was to 'appeal to 30-somethings who grew up with *Doctor Who* but who aren't necessarily devoted fans. This way *Doctor Who* licensing can be a going concern and the business remains alive.' She also explained that they had looked at the existing licences and gone 'through a painful process of deciding which licences to keep and which to part with.'

Dapol, who for many years had been producing low cost toys for the mass market, had already had a request to renew their licence declined. The other two major licences that met a similar fate during this period were those for The Stamp Centre and for Telos Publishing Ltd. The Stamp Centre had been producing items for the nostalgia and collectors' market: signed stamp covers, pewter collectibles, art prints and so on. Telos Publishing Ltd, meanwhile, had been publishing an original range of modern novellas that, on the face of it, seemed to be everything that the BBC wanted from their brand: by using acclaimed genre authors familiar to general science fiction and fantasy readers, Telos were actively trying to broaden interest in *Doctor Who* and bring new readers to the franchise.

Also in 2002, BBC Books decided to halve the number of original *Doctor Who*

Celebrating 40 Years of DOCTOR WHO

DOCTOR WHO

Doctor Who 1963-2003 – 40th Anniversary – Released October 2003
Limited to 3,999 Numbered Boxes Worldwide
36 Packs of 8 Cards Per Pack

DOCTOR WHO 40 1963-2003

12 Gold Foil Premium Cards Per Box
1 Rare Genuine Costume Card Per Box
12 New Gold Foil Cards to Collect
All New Images, 100 Card Thick Double UV Card Set
Covering Every Season, Every Doctor and Every Companion and Much, Much More. The Definitive 4th Collection.

Strictly ink Production

REELTIME PICTURES LAUNCHES INTO DVD...

Our first new title available on DVD and VHS focuses on PATRICK TROUGHTON's tenth touring the USA in the 1980's. Featuring previously unseen and TOTALLY EXCLUSIVE footage, this production follows Patrick's appearances across the states at conventions and on PBS television - NOT TO BE MISSED!

EACH MONTH, Reeltime Pictures will re-releasing TWO classic MYTH MAKERS titles on ONE DVD at the amazing price of only £10.99...

...But you only have one month to get your copy... after that they will revert to the normal retail price of £15.99.

PATRICK TROUGHTON in AMERICA

MYTH MAKERS

VHS £12.99 DVD £15.99

DVD ONLY £10.99 FOR A LIMITED PERIOD

Our first double pack is NICOLA BRYANT and GRAEME HARPER.

Don't forget you only have one month to get your copy at £10.99... after that they will revert to the normal retail price of £15.99.

DON'T MISS THIS AMAZING OPPORTUNITY TO BUILD THE ULTIMATE DOCTOR WHO INTERVIEW SERIES ON DVD AT A FANTASTIC PRICE!

You can buy all Reeltime products from the following stores:
ANDROMEDA BOOKSHOP • GUSTON BOOKS • FORBIDDEN PLANET • GALAXY 4 • KULTURE SHOCK
PURPLE HAZE • SHEFFIELD SPACE CENTRE • TENTH PLANET • WHOSHOP INTERNATIONAL
Or direct from us at...

of the special, additional publishing projects we have coming up.' Then, speaking in 2003, Justin Richards additionally commented: 'The cutback to one a month was partly forced on us by our American distributor going bust, which meant we had a warehouse full of books and there wasn't physical space to store any more. So that was a pragmatic decision which came at a time when we needed people who normally worked on the novels to work on *The Legend* and *The Dalek Survival Guide.*'

The cutback in the frequency of publication of the novels had the undesired effect that an ongoing storyline through the Eighth Doctor books was drawn out over an extended period, leaving some readers frustrated and confused at the direction the range was taking. This may have been a factor

novels that they were publishing. To this point, they had been releasing two novels per month, except in December. There had been eleven novels a year featuring the continuing adventures of the Eighth Doctor, as played by Paul McGann on television, and eleven more featuring new adventures of earlier incarnations. With the decision to cut back, the books reduced to one a month, and alternated between the Eighth Doctor and earlier Doctors.

According to a statement in March 2002 from range editor Ben Dunn and commissioning editor Justin Richards: 'There is a lot of high quality *Doctor Who* merchandise around at the moment, and that's set to increase with the 40th anniversary. We have taken a deliberate decision not to risk over-saturating the market.' They explained that publishing just one novel per month, 'makes room in the schedules – and the pockets – for some

BBC

Doctor Who: The Legend
40 Years of Time Travel
Justin Richard
£40.00
ISBN: 0563486023
The most lavish and comprehensive guide to the longest running sci-fi series ever. Celebrating 40 years of the Doctor's adventures, this book will be packed with behind-the-scenes information and never before seen photographs – a must for any fan.
Pub Date: 13 November

contributing to a reported significant fall in sales of the novels over this period.

Big Finish suffered no such problems; and with 27 original cast dramas on CD released in 2003, fans had a lot to choose from. As well as the 'regular' range of audio releases – which included a Dalek story, adventures featuring the return of three of the most popular characters from the series' past (Davros, Omega and the Master) and a 40th anniversary romp (*Zagreus*), not to mention a musical (*Doctor Who and the Pirates*) and more guest star appearances than you could shake a stick at – there was also a range of 'Unbound' *Doctor Who* adventures. The latter range cast new actors in the role of the Doctor and gave fans a chance to see what the series might have been like given different casting and production decisions along the way. With actors of the calibre of Geoffrey Bayldon, David Warner, David Collings, Michael Jayston, Sir Derek Jacobi and Arabella Weir cast in the title role, expectations were high for the series. Alongside this, there were four more CDs in the *Dalek Empire* series – a spin off range featuring the Daleks, but not the Doctor. These continued the story started in *Dalek War* in 2002, and were reminiscent of the old comic strips and annuals from the sixties, where the Daleks ruled supreme and the Doctor was nowhere in sight.

As if all this product on CD wasn't enough, Big Finish also released four new hardback collections of *Doctor Who* short stories, two new hardback volumes of scripts from their audios, and a lavish, large-format hardback book all about their audio adventures.

If a fan bought all the Big Finish items released in 2003, at recommended retail price, then the total cost would have amounted to just over £410 for the year. And this doesn't take into account the company's Bernice Summerfield audio range, which during 2003 featured some *Doctor Who* monsters, or a CD release of incidental music from their audios.

BBC Worldwide released the second highest number of items in the year. In contrast to the cutbacks in the BBC Books range, the release schedule of *Doctor Who* DVDs increased in pace, with seven titles appearing, one for each Doctor. *The Three Doctors* was also available as a special collectors boxed set, including one of Corgi's Bessie models (see below). The last stories to be released on VHS video also appeared, ending with *The Reign of Terror* in another boxed set,

mopping up the few remaining unreleased individual episodes from incomplete stories along with it. As luck would have it, almost as soon as *The Reign of Terror* hit the shops, another episode was recovered (from *The Daleks' Master Plan*), so there is still one episode yet to be released on video in any form.

The release of *The Reign of Terror* brought to an end an incredible run of *Doctor Who* episodes on video. BBC Worldwide started this release programme back in 1983, and it took 20 years to get to the end of it. Along the way, the design of the video sleeves and packaging was changed several times, so any fans lucky enough to have a complete set would find a distinctly non-uniform collection of releases on their shelves! Hopefully it won't take another 20 years for all the available *Doctor Who* episodes to appear on DVD; however, it already seems likely, from the initial run of titles, that the same problem of lack of uniformity will recur, as the first DVD release (*The Five Doctors*) has a different packaging design from the others. Some things never change!

In the BBC's Radio Collection of audios, the release of 'missing episodes' of *Doctor Who* continued, with two more sixties adventures appearing in this narrated format for the first time, along with re-releases on MP3 CD of some of the back catalogue. New versions of *The Power of the Daleks* and *The Evil of the Daleks* were also released in a popular tin-boxed set, along with a radio documentary entitled *My Life As A Dalek*.

Finally, BBC Books' big anniversary project was a lavish hardbacked book called *The Legend*, which range editor Justin Richards assembled. Retailing at a whopping £40 apiece (although it could be bought at a discount from some retailers, including one online outlet that made copies available for only £16), *The Legend* was certainly impressive, but some fans and commentators were somewhat upset that the novels had been cut back, in part, to allow this book to be produced.

A fan would have had to have spent just over £500 to have picked up all the BBC releases in 2003, which, in addition to the above, included CDs of incidental music and boxed set re-releases of some earlier material.

Taking both Big Finish's and BBC Worldwide's output into account, a collector would have had to fork out around £1000 over the course of the year if they wanted to get everything – an average of £83 each and every month. Unlike in the sixties, when products were squarely aimed at a general market, the majority of the items released in 2003 were aimed at *Doctor Who*'s core fanbase. This was also the market for the many 'collectors' editions' released by nearly all the major companies granted *Doctor Who* licences by BBC Worldwide. Arguably the only product from the BBC or Big Finish that, in terms of its content, sought to find a general, non-fan audience, was *The Legend* book; but, as mentioned above, the product was priced as a specialist buy, and thus anyone casually interested in it would more than likely have been put off. (As a side issue, *The Legend* was supplied to shops sealed in cellophane, so the potential purchaser couldn't even flick through it to see what it was like.)

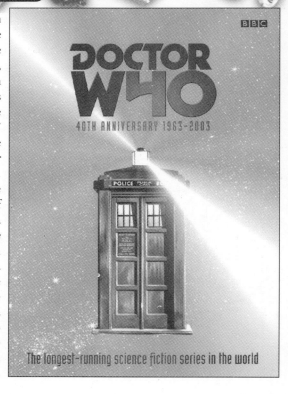

BBC

DOCTOR WHO

40TH ANNIVERSARY 1963-2003

The longest-running science fiction series in the world

Corgi were the recipients of one of two new *Doctor Who* licences to be issued by BBC Worldwide after they culled their existing range. This company was well known for producing metal cars and toys, and their *Doctor Who* range appeared toward the end of 2003, after several delays. Although variable in quality, the toys were well priced, and there were the usual collectors' items produced as well – in this case, a TARDIS boxed set (for The Stamp Centre) and a special film-can set containing one of each of the toys in the range.

The other new licensee was Cards Inc, who produced a range of four ceramic plates celebrating the anniversary and the show – with a fifth one exclusive to The Stamp Centre. In addition, they released a set of five small card standees of selected characters. A range of cookie jars was also advertised, but failed to appear in 2003 – currently these items are promised for release sometime in 2004.

The Stamp Centre, having lost their licence from the BBC in 2002, looked towards the two sixties Dalek cinema films for inspiration, and quickly discovered that Canal+, who own all rights in those films – including their versions of the Daleks and the TARDIS police box – was more than willing to issue licences. Consequently they launched a range of stamp covers and other items featuring the Daleks and other imagery from the films. Product Enterprise also released some film-related items – their inflatable Dalek was notable in that regard – and produced a range of laser etched cubes for The Stamp Centre, again featuring film imagery. The Stamp Centre was, in fact, at the forefront of marketing other people's items, including the above-mentioned special limited editions of some of the Corgi toys and the exclusive Cards Inc plate – although these special editions also tended to be available from other dealers, as The Stamp Centre acted as a supplier for trade as well as selling the items direct themselves.

Product Enterprises expanded their range of talking Daleks with some new colours. In addition to the inflatable movie Dalek (also in two colours), they produced a talking Fourth Doctor and K-9 set in attractive police box packaging. Unfortunately, as 2003 came to an end, they suffered a catastrophic fire in one of their warehouses, and stocks of several items due for despatch to shops were destroyed. Thus the inflatable Dalek and talking Tom Baker and K-9 set did not have as wide a distribution as they might have hoped.

Reeltime Pictures started re-releasing all their interview tapes and dramas on DVD, and their schedule continues. A special DVD and video drama for the 40th anniversary, *Daemos Rising*, did not appear in October as originally slated, and instead was released in March 2004.

Strictly Ink continued with their releases of trading cards, and 2003 saw two new series released. One featured the two Dalek films from the sixties, and the other was a 40th anniversary set. The Strickly Ink sets have been notable for their impressive range of autograph cards, and these latest two did not disappoint in this regard.

Telos Publishing, although having been told in August 2002 that their *Doctor Who* novellas licence was not to be renewed, still had until March 2004 to continue to bring out new titles. They added a further eight to the range (including an almost obligatory collectors' edition of their anniversary book, Paul McAuley's *The Eye of the Tyger*) in 2003. Of the eight novellas published, three were by authors (Louise Cooper, Mark Chadbourn and Paul McAuley) who had not previously been involved in *Doctor Who* work. To pen forewords to the novellas, Telos Publishing commissioned some big-name authors from the general science fiction and fantasy mainstream: Stephen Gallagher, Stephen Laws, Storm Constantine, Neil Gaiman, Guy N Smith, Chaz Brenchley and Graham Joyce.

Telos Publishing also released an

updated edition of *The Television Companion*. BBC Books had decided in 2002 to remainder (i.e. sell off any remaining stocks and make unavailable) its official television series guide, *Doctor Who: The Television Companion*. The rights to the title had then reverted to the authors, David J Howe and Stephen James Walker, and they had been only too pleased to release a revised and updated version of the book through Telos Publishing for the anniversary.

In fact, there were three different episode guides released in 2003, all unofficial in that they were not licensed by the BBC. *The Television Companion* is referred to as 'the *Doctor Who* bible' by some fans, and this was, at 752 pages, the biggest and most comprehensive of the books as far as documenting the television series went. The other two were both by Mark Campbell. *Dimensions in Time and Space* was released by The Stamp Centre and covered not only the TV series but also the books, audios and other spin-offs. This came in at 360 pages. The final reference work was a revised and updated edition of the slim Pocket Essentials guide to *Doctor Who*. At only 96 pages, this is really only a brief skim through the show but manages to list the audios and spin offs as well.

Doctor Who Magazine continued to appear every four weeks under the editorship of Clayton Hickman (who was also kept busy creating covers for the BBC's DVD range and the occasional cover for Big Finish's range of CDs). Andrew Pixley's impressive Archives

feature came to a natural end in June with coverage of *The Mutants* (1963/4). Further Archives on *The Curse of Fatal Death*, the 1977 *Whose Doctor Who* documentary and the 1993 documentary *30 Years in the TARDIS* were also included. Regular features were the news pages (Gallifrey Guardian), the reviews, previews of new Big Finish audios, BBC novels and DVD releases and Telos novellas. Articles presented throughout the year included: looking at the man behind the Time Lord (from Gareth Roberts), what makes a fan a fan (by Gary Gillatt), the Dalek War series from Big Finish, Mary Whitehouse and the Viewers and Listeners Association, The Sarah Jane Smith series from Big Finish, Big Finish and BBCi's audio dramatisation of Douglas Adams' *Shada*, the limited number of

story ideas in *Doctor Who* (by Gareth Roberts), a new series called 'The Fact of Fiction' to replace the Archives looking at the historical facts behind some of the stories (*The Deadly Assassin*, *Invasion of the Dinosaurs*, *100,000 BC*), 'The Accidental Tourist' – articles looking at the development of the series by Daniel O'Mahony, a *Blue Peter*-themed issue by Andrew Pixley, behind the scenes on the BBCi webcast cartoon *Scream of the Shalka*, a look at the work of the BBC Radio Collection, and behind the scenes on Big Finish's 40th anniversary audio play *Zagreus*.

Interviews formed the usual strong element in *Doctor Who* Magazine's mix, and people spoken to over the course of the year included sixth Doctor Colin Baker, jazz musician Courtney Pine, Richard Briars, Martin Jarvis, writer of *Kinda* and *Snakedance* Christopher Bailey (in his first ever interview), book author Kate Orman, David Collings, Lisa Goddard, musician and composer Dudley Simpson, book authors Mike Tucker and Robert Perry, actor and writer Mark Gatiss, Sarah Greene, Janet Ellis, Peter Miles, Paul McGann, and producer and writer Barry Letts and script editor and writer Terrance Dicks.

Doctor Who Magazine continued to look fresh and new each issue, and Panini also brought out several themed special magazines in the course of the year. There were specials devoted to individual Doctors, and one celebrating the 40th anniversary.

Overall, *Doctor Who* fans were well served, if not downright spoilt, by the sheer variety and expanse of new material in the 40th anniversary year. As well as all the commercially available products listed here, there were also webcasts from BBCi, including the aforementioned new animated adventure, *Scream of the Shalka*, which starred Richard E Grant as the Doctor. There were masses of new adventures from BBC Books, Big Finish and Telos Publishing, loads of old *Doctor Who* adventures to enjoy again on video, audio and DVD courtesy of various arms of BBC Worldwide, and a lot of optimism about the future of *Doctor Who*, which was proving, as it had done several times previously, to be a brand that survives against all the odds.

TOP 20 MOST VALUABLE WHO COLLECTIBLES

THE one question we hear most often at conventions and online is "What is the most valuable *Doctor Who* collectible ever made?" Herewith we present our first-ever Top Twenty Most Valuable *Who* Collectibles list, culling data from throughout the second edition of the main *Toybox* volume. Keep in mind though that value does not necessarily equal rarity.

1. PINBALL MACHINE (GAR-003A)

While not all that rare or difficult to obtain (several of them are on eBay at almost any given moment), the average sale price and sheer size of the item makes the Bally *Doctor Who* pinball machine a true Holy Grail for the dedicated *Who* collector. Second stage!
Toybox Value: £3250

2. FRUIT MACHINE (GAR-004)

Certainly a much rarer item and almost never to be found outside the UK, the Fruit Machine by Bell is a perfect complement to the pinball machine if you're the type that doesn't mind spending thousands of pounds and then taking up most of your living room with huge arcade games.
Toybox Value: £2250

3. THIS PLANET EARTH DALEKS/TARDIS (COL-009, 037)

What better way to say you're a true blue fan of the Doctor and his adventures than to buy your very own exact full-size replica of his TARDIS and his deadliest foes? The TV TARDIS has been discontinued, but if you hurry, you can still buy a Cushing movie-style police box.
Toybox Value: Daleks £1600-2000; TARDIS £1000-2000

4. FULL-SIZE CYBERMAN/CYBERMAN SUITS (COL-039)

It's not strictly traditional formal wear, but you'll make an impression, that's for sure. Two different manufacturers have offered the suits, so there must be quite a silver-coated fashion phenomenon out there.
Toybox Value: MAKE Full-Size £1695; This Planet Earth Cyberman £800-1600

5. HIRSCHFELD LITHOGRAPH (COL-007)

Al Hirschfeld was one of the greatest illustrators that ever lived, making his mark on the histories of film, television, stage, and radio with his unerringly accurate caricatures of the men and women who made up the US's media elite. This was a stunning tribute and one of his rarer pieces.
Toybox Value: $1500

6. DALEK PLAYSUIT ⟨TYG-001⟩

One of the legends of *Who* collecting. By now most of us know the story of the warehouse fire that hit just before Christmas 1965, leaving Scorpion Automotives without stock at the busiest time of year. This event was eerily paralleled in 2003 when Product Enterprise experienced a similar crisis. *Toybox* Value: £1350

7. DALEK KIDDIE RIDE/TARDIS KIDDIE RIDE ⟨GAR-001, 002⟩

A tough pair of large-size collectibles to obtain, not least because they were meant to be treated roughly in outdoor venues by children who hopped in for a quick bumpy ride in a police box or Skarosian invader. Also rarely found outside the UK. *Toybox* Value: Each £1100

8. SONTARAN COSTUME ⟨MGA-022⟩

So the Cyberman gear didn't work for you? Then how about dressing up as one of those potato-headed clones with the military fixation and the quilted armour? It's a pricey way to say you're a fan, but no one will forget you – just make sure you keep the back of your neck covered. *Toybox* Value: £999.99

PICTURE
NOT
AVAILABLE

9. FULL-SIZE K9 ⟨COL-038⟩

Now discontinued, the K9 (with motorised option) was one of the This Planet Earth's most accurate and most popular collectibles. Just a tad more affordable than a Dalek or a TARDIS, the reproduction K9 offered every fan the chance to own their own second best friend. *Toybox* Value: £795

10. CHESS SET ⟨COL-010⟩

Still a highly sought-after set in its entirety, this stunning array of pewter figurines by MBI spanned the history of *Who* and also included two expansion sets with characters from the 1996 TV movie and more monsters. Even individual pieces fetch a premium, but a full set is a *Who* holy grail. *Toybox* Value: £625

11. CLOCKWORK DALEK ⟨TYG-009⟩

Now that Product Enterprise have released their own clockwork Dalek in homage to the original Cowan de Groot collectible, demand for the 1965 model is on the rise. While he's less accurate in proportion than the new effort, this little guy remains one of the icons of '60s Dalekmania. *Toybox* Value: £600

PICTURE NOT AVAILABLE

12. TARDIS CLIMBING FRAME (HGE-004)

Only twelve of these, made by Furitubes Associated Products, were known to be distributed.
Toybox Value: £550

13. HALF-SIZE DALEK (COL-049)

Tell your friends you bought a This Planet Earth full-size Dalek and blasted it with a shrink ray to make this Daleks Direct item.
Toybox Value: £500

14. ASTRO RAY GUN (TYG-031)

This Dalek item from Bell Toys is another '60s icon and has significant crossover appeal with collectors who focus on acquiring vintage toy guns.
Toybox Value: £440

15. DALEK SHOOTING GAME (TYG-022)

What could be more fun than encouraging children to fire weapons at vicious alien invaders? That's the theme of this '60s Louis Marx game.
Toybox Value: £400

16. DALEK SLIPPERS (CCM-002)

It's hard to maintain your dignity when you're shuffling around in these bright red booties with the Daleks on from Furness Footwear.
Toybox Value: £400

17. DALEK PLAYSUIT (TYG-020)

While not as rare or expensive as the Scorpion model, this *other* 1965 Dalek playsuit from Berwick Toy Co. is still highly desirable.
Toybox Value: £375

18. MECHANOID (LARGE) (TYG-042)

The Mechanoids never caught on like their predecessors, the Daleks, but merchandise makers like Hertz Plastic Moulders certainly tried their best.
Toybox Value: £375

19. DALEK ORACLE/DALEK GLOVE PUPPET (TYG-019, 008)

Both are valuable '60s Dalek items (from Bell Toys and Newfeld Ltd respectively), although the Oracle game is far more likely to be found.
Toybox Value: Each £350

20. DENYS FISHER ROBOT (TYA-004)

Arguably the centrepiece of a Denys Fisher *Who* collection, the Giant Robot is often incomplete, with missing shoulder pads and/or internal rubber band.
Toybox Value: £325

2003 TOYBOX ITEM LISTINGS

AAP-009 (Tom Baker, Colin Baker and Sylvester McCoy shown)

AAP-010

ABF-040

ARTIST PROMOTIONAL ITEMS

AAP-009 Character Laser Etched Cubes
2003, The Stamp Centre, UK
Laser etched blocks with an actor's image inside.
Designs: Tom Baker, Colin Baker, Sylvester McCoy,
Nicholas Courtney, Louise Jameson. Comes in a pres-
entation box. Limited to 1500 of each.
OP: £49.50 each

AAP-010 Colin Baker Stamp Cover
2003/07, The Stamp Centre, UK
First of a new series called 'Time after Time' showing
Doctor Who stars as they were and as they are now.
OP: £14.95

AUDIO, BIG FINISH DRAMAS

IN 2003, Big Finish celebrated *Doctor Who*'s 40th
anniversary with the release of their 50th *Doctor
Who* audio drama, a triple CD story, *Zagreus,* featuring a plethora of *Who* actors and one surprise
guest star. Big Finish's audio dramas are edited by
Gary Russell, with Jac Rayner acting as BBC
Worldwide's Executive Producer on the range.

ABF-040 *Doctor Who: Jubilee* (Robert Shearman)
2003/01, Big Finish Productions, UK
Twin CD. Features the Daleks. Cover by Clayton
Hickman. Starring Colin Baker. CD has the more cor-
rect code BFPDWCD7CG on it.
REF: BFPCD7CG OP: £13.99

**ABF-041 *Doctor Who:Nekromanteia* (Austen
Atkinson)**
2003/02, Big Finish Productions, UK
Twin CD. Cover by Lee Binding. Starring Peter
Davison and Nicola Bryant.
REF: BFPDWCD6QD OP: £13.99

ABF-041

ABF-042 *Doctor Who: The Dark Flame* (Trevor Baxendale)
2003/03, Big Finish Productions, UK
Twin CD. Cover by Lee Binding. Starring Sylvester McCoy and Sophie Aldred.
REF: BFPDWCDSS4 OP: £13.99

ABF-043 *Doctor Who and the Pirates* (Jacqueline Rayner)
2003/04, Big Finish Productions, UK
Twin CD. Cover by Lee Binding. Starring Colin Baker.
CD is subtitled, *or The Lass That Lost A Sailor.*
REF: BFPDWCD7CH OP: £13.99

ABF-044 *Doctor Who: Creatures of Beauty* (Nicholas Briggs)
2003/05, Big Finish Productions, UK
Twin CD. Cover by Paul Burley. Starring Peter Davison and Sarah Sutton.
REF: BFPDWCD6CF OP: £13.99

ABF-045 *Doctor Who: Project: Lazarus* (Cavan Scott and Mark Wright)
2003/06, Big Finish Productions, UK
Twin CD. Cover by Lee Binding. Starring Colin Baker and Sylvester McCoy. CD issued with two different covers, one featuring Baker and one featuring McCoy.
REF: BFPDWCD7CJ7X OP: £13.99

ABF-042

ABF-043

ABF-044

ABF-045
(Baker cover)

ABF-045
(McCoy cover)

ABF-046

ABF-047

ABF-048

ABF-049

ABF-046 *Doctor Who: Flip Flop* **(Jonathan Morris)**
2003/07, Big Finish Productions, UK
Twin CD. Cover by Lee Binding. Starring Sylvester
McCoy and Bonnie Langford. CDs issued in separate
plastic cases, and with a card slipcase.
REF: BFPDWCD7EB OP: £13.99

ABF-047 *Doctor Who: Omega* **(Nev Fountain)**
2003/08, Big Finish Productions, UK
Twin CD. Cover by Clayton Hickman. Starring Peter
Davison and Ian Collier as Omega.
REF: BFPDWCD6EA OP: £13.99

ABF-048 *Doctor Who: Davros* **(Lance Parkin)**
2003/09, Big Finish Productions, UK
Twin CD. Cover by Clayton Hickman. Starring Colin
Baker and Terry Molloy as Davros.
REF: BFPDWCD6WA OP: £13.99

ABF-049 *Doctor Who: Master* **(Joseph Lidster)**
2003/10, Big Finish Productions, UK
Twin CD. Cover by Clayton Hickman. Starring
Sylvester McCoy and Geoffrey Beevers as the Master.
REF: BFPDWCD7Y OP: £13.99

ABF-050 *Doctor Who: Zagreus* **(Alan Barnes
and Gary Russell)**
2003/11, Big Finish Productions, UK
Triple CD. Cover by Clayton Hickman. Starring Peter
Davison, Colin Baker, Sylvester McCoy and Paul McGann.
With Nicholas Courtney, Lalla Ward, Louise Jameson and
John Leeson. The surprise guest star is Jon Pertwee, in
material taken from an unreleased fan-produced audio
drama made before the actor's death in 1996.
REF: BFPDWCD8M OP: £13.99

ABF-050

ABF-051

ABF-051 *Doctor Who: The Wormery* **(Stephen Cole and Paul Magrs)**
2003/11, Big Finish Productions, UK
Twin CD. Cover by Lee Binding. Starring Colin Baker.
REF: BFPDWCDSS5 OP: £13.99

ABF-052 *Doctor Who: Scherzo* **(Robert Shearman)**
2003/12, Big Finish Productions, UK
Twin CD. Cover by Steve Johnson. Starring Paul McGann.
REF: BFPDWCD8N OP: £13.99

ABF-052

AUDIO DRAMAS

ADR-010 *Doctor Who: Unbound: Auld Mortality* **(Marc Platt)**
2003/05, Big Finish Productions, UK
Single CD. Cover by Clayton Hickman. Starring Geoffrey Bayldon as the Doctor and Carole Ann Ford as Susan. The *Unbound* range of CDs presented 'alternate' Doctors to those seen on television.
REF: BFPDWUNCD01 OP: £9.99

ADR-011 *Doctor Who: Unbound: Sympathy for the Devil* **(Jonathan Clements)**
2003/06, Big Finish Productions, UK
Single CD. Cover by Clayton Hickman. Starring David Warner as the Doctor and Nicholas Courtney as the Brigadier.
REF: BFPDWUNCD02 OP: £9.99

ADR-010

ADR-011

ADR-012

ADR-013

ADR-014

ADR-012 *Doctor Who: Unbound: Full Fathom Five* **(David Bishop)**
2003/07, Big Finish Productions, UK
Single CD. Cover by Clayton Hickman. Starring David Collings as the Doctor.
REF: BFPDWUNCD03 OP: £9.99

ADR-013 *Doctor Who: Unbound:He Jests At Scars* **(Gary Russell)**
2003/08, Big Finish Productions, UK
Single CD. Cover by Clayton Hickman. Starring Michael Jayston as the Valeyard and Bonnie Langford as Mel.
REF: BFPDWUNCD04 OP: £9.99

ADR-014 *Doctor Who: Unbound:Deadline* **(Robert Shearman)**
2003/09, Big Finish Productions, UK
Single CD. Cover by Clayton Hickman. Starring Sir Derek Jacobi as Martin.
REF: BFPDWUNCD05 OP: £9.99

ADR-015 *Doctor Who: Unbound:Exile* **(Nicholas Briggs)**
2003/10, Big Finish Productions, UK
Single CD. Cover by Clayton Hickman. Starring Arabella Weir as the Doctor and Nicholas Briggs as the previous Doctor.
REF: BFPDWUNCD06 OP: £9.99

ADR-016 *Doctor Who: Shada* **(Douglas Adams)**
2003/12, Big Finish Productions, UK
Twin CD. Cover by Clayton Hickman. Starring Paul McGann. Release of a story originally presented as a webcast on the BBCi website.
REF: BFPDWBBCiCD02 OP: £13.99

AUDIO DRAMA SPIN-OFFS

ADS-013 *Kaldor City: Taran Kapel* **(Alan Stevens)**
2003/03/15, Magic Bullet, UK
CD. Cover by Andy Hopkinson. Story features characters and situations from *The Robots of Death*. Fourth in the series.
REF: KC004 OP: £10.99

ADS-014 *Kaldor City: Checkmate* **(Alan Stevens)**
2003/11, Magic Bullet, UK
CD. Cover by Andy Hopkinson. Story features characters and situations from *The Robots of Death*. Fifth in the series.
REF: KC005 OP: £10.99

ADS-015 *Dalek Empire II: Dalek War Chapter One* **(Nicholas Briggs)**
2003/01, Big Finish Productions, UK
CD. Cover by Clayton Hickman. Story features the Daleks in a sequel to the previous year's *Dalek Empire* series.
REF: BFPCDDE05 OP: £9.99

ADS-016 *Dalek Empire II: Dalek War Chapter Two* **(Nicholas Briggs)**
2003/02, Big Finish Productions, UK
CD. Cover by Clayton Hickman.
REF: BFPCDDE06 OP: £9.99

ADR-015

ADR-016

ADS-013

ADS-014

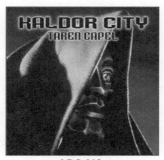

ADS-015

ADS-016

ADS-017

ADS-018

AMU-029a

AOT-018

ADS-017 *Dalek Empire II:Dalek War Chapter Three* **(Nicholas Briggs)**
2003/03, Big Finish Productions, UK
CD. Cover by Clayton Hickman.
REF: BFPCDDE07 OP: £9.99

ADS-018 *Dalek Empire II:Dalek War Chapter Four* **(Nicholas Briggs)**
2003/04, Big Finish Productions, UK
CD. Cover by Clayton Hickman.
REF: BFPCDDE08 OP: £9.99

AUDIO, MUSIC

AMU-029a *Doctor Who: Devils' Planets: The Music of Tristram Cary*
2003/09/01, BBC Music, UK
Double CD. Photographic cover. Music by Tristram Cary from the *Doctor Who* stories: *The Mutants* (1963/4), *The Daleks' Master Plan* and *The Mutants* (1972).
REF: WMSF 6072-2 OP: £16.99

AMU-029b *Doctor Who: Devils' Planets: The Music of Tristram Cary*
2003/12/03, ABC, AUS
REF: 300880-2 OP: $21.99

AUDIO, OTHER

AOT-018 *Doctor Who: Music from the Seventh Doctor Audio Adventures*
2003/04, Big Finish Productions, UK
CD. Music by Russell Stone (*Dust Breeding*), Jim Mortimore (*The Rapture*) and Andy Hardwick (*Bang-Bang-a-Boom*).
REF: BFPCDMUSIC8 OP: £9.99

AOT-019a

AST-017b

AST-022

AOT-019a *Doctor Who at the BBC*
2003/09/01, BBC Worldwide Ltd, UK
Double CD. *Doctor Who* material from the BBC Radio archives. Presented by Elisabeth Sladen.
Track List: CD 1: *30 Years* (BBC Radio 2, 20 November 1993); CD 2: *Today* (BBC Radio 4, 8 January 1973); *Sunday Best* (BBC Radio 4, 6 February 1972); *Today* (BBC Radio 4, 28 March 1972); *Profile* (BBC World Service, April 1974); *Morning Sou'West* (BBC Radio 4 South West, 30 September 1974); *Exploration Earth* (BBC Radio 4, 4 October 1976); *The Paradise of Death* (BBC Radio 5, 10 September 1993); *Pete Murray's Open House* (BBC Radio 2, 29 August 1978); *Today* (BBC Radio 4, 9 October 1980); *The Ed Stewart Show* (BBC Radio 2, 4 April 1983); *The Enthusiasts* (BBC Radio 4, 11 December 1985); *Hello Cheeky* (BBC Radio 2, 21 April 1973); *Week Ending* (BBC Radio 4, 30 November 1990); *The Skivers* (BBC Radio 4, 23 February 1995); *Newsbeat 12:30* (BBC Radio 1, 10 February 1999); *Today* (BBC Radio 4, 13 November 1999); *Dead Ringers* (BBC Radio 4, 7 January 2000); *Blue Veils and Golden Sands* (BBC Radio 4, 23 December 2002).
REF: ISBN 0-563-53087-1 OP: £13.99

AUDIO, SOUNDTRACKS

AST-017b Doctor Who: *The Daleks' Master Plan*
2003/04/07, BBC Worldwide Ltd, UK
MP3-CD Audio release.
REF: ISBN 0-563-49417-4 OP: £19.99

AST-022 Doctor Who: *The Space Pirates*
2003/02/03, BBC Worldwide Ltd, UK
Double CD. Cover by Max Ellis. Narrated by Frazer Hines.
REF: ISBN 0-563-53505-9 OP: £13.99

AST-023 Doctor Who: *The Abominable Snowmen* and *The Web of Fear*
2003/04/07, BBC Worldwide Ltd, UK
MP3-CD Audio release. See also AST-016 and AST-009.
REF: ISBN 0-563-49417-4 OP: £19.99

AST-023

AST-024

AST-025

AST-026

AST-027

ATH-013

AST-024 Doctor Who: Yeti Attack

2003/07/07, BBC Worldwide Ltd, UK
Boxed set of *The Web of Fear* and *The Abominable Snowmen*. Box illustration by Bill Sanderson. See also AST-009 and AST-016.
REF: ISBN 0-563-49535-9 OP: £24.99

AST-025 Doctor Who: Adventures in History

2003/08/04, BBC Worldwide Ltd, UK
Boxed set of *The Myth Makers, The Massacre* and *The Highlanders*. Box illustration by Bill Sanderson. See also AST-013, AST-008, and AST-011.
REF: ISBN 0-563-49494-8 OP: £29.99

AST-026 Dalek Tin

2003/11/03, BBC Worldwide Ltd, UK
Metal tin containing remastered audio CDs of *The Power of the Daleks* and *The Evil of the Daleks*. With new narration by Anneke Wills and Frazer Hines respectively. Also includes the Mark Gatiss-presented radio documentary *My Life as a Dalek*. See AST-003 and AST-006. Tin illustrations by Max Ellis (2003) and Victor Reinganum (1968). This tin sold out in early 2004.
REF: ISBN 0-563-49476-X OP: £29.99

AST-027 Doctor Who: *Marco Polo*

2003/11/03, BBC Worldwide Ltd, UK
Triple CD. Cover by Max Ellis. Narrated by William Russell. The first disk contains MP3 files of the episodes without narration. The CD also features a fold out map of Polo's journey.
REF: ISBN 0-563-53508-3 OP: £16.99

AUDIO, THEMES

ATH-013 *resistance is futile: doctor who remixed*

2003/11/01, UK
A promotional CD for a forthcoming remix album given away free to attendees at the 2003 Panopticon convention in London on 1st and 2nd November 2003.
OP: free

AUDIO, UNLICENSED

AUN-016 *Bernice Summerfield and the Dance of the Dead* **(Stephen Cole)**
2002/10/22, Big Finish Productions, UK
Single CD. Cover by Adrian Salmon. Features the Ice Warriors.
REF: BFPCD14 OP: £9.99

AUN-016

AUN-017 *In 2 Minds* **(Iain Hepburn)**
2003/02, BBV, UK
Single CD. Features the Rutans.
OP: £8.99

AUN-018 *Bernice Summerfield and the Bellotron Incident* **(Mike Tucker)**
2003/04, Big Finish Productions, UK
Single CD. Cover by Adrian Salmon. Features the Rutans.
REF: BFPCD16 OP: £9.99

AUN-017

AUN-019 *The Nightmare Fair* **(Graham Williams)**
2003/05/26, An Argolis Production, UK
Double CD. Cover by Ryan O'Neill. An unofficial adaptation of a 'lost' Season 23 story by Graham Williams. This is a full cast dramatisation with actors Steve Hill and Jennifer Adams Kelley doing impressions of the Sixth Doctor and Peri. Raising money for the Scope charity.
REF: None OP: £6.00

AUN-020 *Bernice Summerfield and the Draconian Rage* **(Trevor Baxendale)**
2003/08, Big Finish Productions, UK
Single CD. Cover by Adrian Salmon. Features the Draconians.
REF: BFPCD17 OP: £9.99

AUN-018

AUN-021 *Bernice Summerfield and the Poison Seas* **(David Bailey)**
2003/09, Big Finish Productions, UK
Single CD. Cover by Adrian Salmon. Features the Sea Devils.
REF: BFPCD18 OP: £9.99

AUN-019

AUN-020

AUN-021

BAT-016

BAT-017

BAT-018

BOOKS, ANTHOLOGIES

BIG Finish, makers of the licensed *Doctor Who* audio dramas, now continue (under licence) the anthology umbrella title, *Short Trips*, originally employed by BBC Books for its own *Who* short story anthologies.

BAT-016 *Doctor Who: Short Trips Companions* (ed. Jacqueline Rayner)
2003/03, Big Finish Productions, UK
Anthology of stories themed around the Doctor's companions. Cover by Clayton Hickman. Range editors: Gary Russell and Ian Farrington. Managing editor: Jason Haigh-Ellery.
Stories: *The Tip of the Mind* (Peter Anghelides); *The Splintered Gate* (Justin Richards); *The Man from DOCTO(R)* (Andrew Collins); *Apocrypha Bipedium* (Ian Potter); *A Boy's Tale* (Gary Russell); *Kept Safe and Sound* (Paul Magrs); *The Lying Old Witch in the Wardrobe* (Mark Michalowski); *Hearts of Stone* (Steve Lyons); *Distance* (Tara Samms); *Qualia* (Stephen Frewell); *Curriculum Vitae* (Simon Guerrier); *Notre Dame Du Temps* (Nick Clark); *The Little Drummer Boy* (Eddie Robson); *Hidden Talent* (Andrew Spokes); *The Canvey Angels* (David Bailey); *Balloon Debate* (Simon A Forward); *A Long Night* (Alison Lawson).
REF: ISBN 1-84435-007-X OP: £14.99 h/b

BAT-017 *Doctor Who: Short Trips A Universe of Terrors* (ed. John Binns)
2003/06, Big Finish Productions, UK
Anthology of stories themed around fears. Cover by Red Ink. Range editors: Gary Russell and Ian Farrington. Managing editor: Jason Haigh-Ellery.
Stories: *The Exiles* (Lance Parkin); *Mire and Clay* (Gareth Wigmore); *Ash* (Trevor Baxendale); *Face-Painter* (Tara Samms); *Losing Track of Time* (Juliet E McKenna); *The Discourse of Files* (Jeremy Daw); *The Fear* (Alexander Leithes); *Mauritz* (Jonathan Morris); *The Comet's Tail* (John Binns); *Long Term* (Andy Campbell); *Soul Mate* (David Bailey); *Whiskey and Water* (Marc Platt); *The Death of Me* (Robert Shearman); *This is My Life* (The seventh Doctor, as told to William Keith); *Gazing Void* (Huw Wilkins).
REF: ISBN 1-84435-008-8 OP: £14.99 h/b

BAT-018 *Doctor Who: Short Trips: The Muses* (ed. Jacqueline Rayner)
2003/09, Big Finish Productions, UK
Anthology of stories themed around the nine Muses. Cover by Red Ink. Range editors: Gary Russell and Ian Farrington. Managing editor: Jason Haigh-Ellery.
Stories: *Tepsichore: Teach Yourself Ballroom Dancing* (Robert Shearman); *Thalia: The Brain of Socrates* (Gareth

Roberts); *Melpomene: Mordieu* (Tara Samms); *Euterpe: An Overture Too Early* (Simon Guerrier); *Polyhymnia: Hymn of the City* (Sara Groenewegen); *Erato: Confabula* (Ian Potter); *Urania: The Astronomer's Apprentice* (Simon A Forward); *Calliope: Katarina in the Underworld* (Steve Lyons); *Clio: The Glass Princess* (Justin Richards).
REF: ISBN 1-84435-009-6 OP: £14.99 h/b

BAT-019 *Doctor Who: Short Trips: Steel Skies* (ed. John Binns)
2003/12, Big Finish Productions, UK
Anthology of stories. Cover by Red Ink. Range editors: Gary Russell and Ian Farrington. Managing editor: Jason Haigh-Ellery.
Stories: *Corridors of Power* (Matthew Griffiths); *A Good Life* (Simon Guerrier); *Reversal of Fortune* (Graeme Burk); *Monitor* (Huw Wilkins); *Dust* (Paul Leonard); *Light at the End of the Tunnel* (Mark Wright); *No Exit* (Kate Orman); *House* (Jeremy Daw); *Deep Stretch* (Richard Salter); *Inmate 280* (Cavan Scott); *Doing Time* (Lance Parkin); *The Ruins of Heaven* (Marc Platt); *Cold War* (Rebecca Levene); *O, Darkness* (John Binns); *Greenaway* (Peter Anghelides); *Eternity* (Jonathan Blum).
REF: ISBN 1-84435-045-2 OP: £14.99 h/b

BAT-019

BOOKS, BBC 8TH DOCTOR

THROUGHOUT the anniversary year of 2003, the BBC released one *Doctor Who* novel a month, alternating between Eighth Doctor and Past Doctor novels.

BBE-062 *Doctor Who: The Domino Effect* (David Bishop)
2003/02/03, BBC Worldwide Ltd, UK
Cover by Black Sheep.
REF: ISBN 0-563-53869-4 OP: £5.99 p/b

BBE-063 *Doctor Who: Reckless Engineering* (Nick Walters)
2003/04/07, BBC Worldwide Ltd, UK
Cover by Black Sheep.
REF: ISBN 0-563-48603-1 OP: £5.99 p/b

BBE-064 *Doctor Who: The Last Resort* (Paul Leonard)
2003/06/02, BBC Worldwide Ltd, UK
Cover by Black Sheep.
REF: ISBN 0-563-48605-8 OP: £5.99 p/b

BBE-065 *Doctor Who: Timeless* (Stephen Cole)
2003/08/04, BBC Worldwide Ltd, UK
Cover by Black Sheep.
REF: ISBN 0-563-48607-4 OP: £5.99 p/b

BBE-062

BBE-063

BBE-064

BBE-065

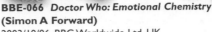

BBE-066

BBE-066 *Doctor Who: Emotional Chemistry*
(Simon A Forward)
2003/10/06, BBC Worldwide Ltd, UK
Cover by Black Sheep.
REF: ISBN 0-563-48608-2 OP: £5.99 p/b

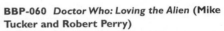
BOOKS, BBC PAST DOCTORS

BBP-058 *Doctor Who: Fear of the Dark* (Trevor
Baxendale)
2003/01/06, BBC Worldwide Ltd, UK
Dr 5.
REF: ISBN 0-563-53865-1 OP: £5.99 p/b

BBP-059 *Doctor Who: Blue Box* (Kate Orman)
2003/03/03, BBC Worldwide Ltd, UK
Dr 6.
REF: ISBN 0-563-53859-7 OP: £5.99 p/b

BBP-060 *Doctor Who: Loving the Alien* (Mike
Tucker and Robert Perry)
2003/05/05, BBC Worldwide Ltd, UK
Dr 7.
REF: ISBN 0-563-48604-X OP: £5.99 p/b

BBP-061 *Doctor Who: Colony of Lies* (Colin
Brake)
2003/07/07, BBC Worldwide Ltd, UK
Dr 2.
REF: ISBN 0-563-48606-6 OP: £5.99 p/b

BBP-062 *Doctor Who: Wolfsbane* (Jacqueline
Rayner)
2003/09/01, BBC Worldwide Ltd, UK
Drs 4 and 8.
REF: ISBN 0-563-48609-0 OP: £5.99 p/b

BBP-058   **BBP-059**

BBP-060   **BBP-061**   **BBP-062**

BBP-063 *Doctor Who: Deadly Reunion*
(Terrance Dicks and Barry Letts)
2003/11/03, BBC Worldwide Ltd, UK
Dr 3.
REF: ISBN 0-563-48610-4 OP: £5.99 p/b

BOOKS, FACTUAL

BFA-005e *The Doctor Who Programme Guide*
(Jean-Marc and Randy Lofficier)
2003/05/08, iUniverse, USA
Slightly updated edition. The text is primarily repro-
duced from the last Virgin edition, with an additional
entry for the Paul McGann TV Movie.
REF: ISBN 0-595-27618-0 OP: $17.95 p/b

BFA-086b *The Nth Doctor* **(Jean-Marc and**
Randy Lofficier)
2003/04/20, iUniverse, USA
Reprint edition.
REF: ISBN 0-595-27619-9 OP: $19.95 p/b

BFA-089b *The Television Companion: The*
Unofficial and Unauthorised Guide to Doctor Who
(David J Howe and Stephen James Walker)
2003/11, Telos Publishing Ltd, UK
New revised and updated edition of the complete
guide to the TV series. Hardback edition was signed
and numbered and limited to 200 copies.
REF: ISBN 1-903889-51-0 p/b; ISBN 1-903889-52-9 h/b
OP: £14.99 p/b; £30.00 h/b

BFA-100b *The Pocket Essential: Doctor Who*
(Mark Campbell)
2003/11, Pocket Essentials, UK
Revised and updated edition. Appears to be the 4th
printing of the book.
REF: ISBN 1-903047-19-6 OP: £3.99 p/b

BBP-063

BFA-005e   **BFA-086b**

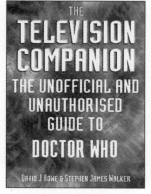

BFA-089b (paperback)   **BFA-089b (hardback)**   **BFA-100b**

BFA-104b

BFA-112

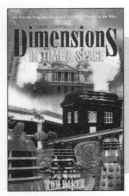

BFA-113

BFA-114

BFA-104b *Howe's Transcendental Toybox*: **Second Edition (David J Howe and Arnold T Blumberg)**
2003/11, Telos Publishing, UK
Cover by Nathan Skreslet and Dariusz Jasiczak. The second edition of the *Doctor Who* merchandise guide. This edition, when ordered from the publishers, came with a limited edition chromed Gunner Rolykin Dalek toy (see TYG-083j). Covers all merchandise from 1963 to the end of 2002.
REF: ISBN 1-903889-56-1 OP: £25.00 p/b

BFA-112 *I, Who 3* **(Lars Pearson)**
2003/06/25, Mad Norwegian Press, USA
Cover by Gene Ha. Edited by Chris Lawrence. Third volume in the *I, Who* series. This edition covers the BBC EDA novels from *Earthworld* to *Time Zero*; the BBC PDA novels from *Rags* to *Ten Little Indians*, plus the Telos novellas, Big Finish audio CDs and other related items.
REF: ISBN 0-9725959-1-0 OP: $21.95 p/b

BFA-113 *Mark Campbell's Dimensions in Time & Space* **(Mark Campbell)**
2003/10, Steven Scott, UK
Cover Canal+ Image. Introduction by Tom Baker. Guide to the TV series and some associated spin offs.
REF: ISBN 1-871330-58-0 OP: £14.95

BFA-114 *Doctor Who: The Legend* **(Justin Richards)**
2003/11/06, BBC Books, UK
Cover by Whereforeart! Lavish hardcover celebrating the 40th anniversary of *Doctor Who*.
REF: ISBN 0-563-48602-3 OP: £40.00 h/b

BFA-115 *Doctor Who: The New Audio Adventures: The Inside Story* **(Benjamin Cook)**
2003/11, Big Finish Productions, UK
Cover by Red Ink. Foreword by Russell T Davies.
Guide to the Big Finish Audio Adventures.
REF: ISBN 1-88435-034-7 OP: £24.99 h/b

BFA-115

BOOKS, JUNIOR

BJU-003b *K9 and the Time Trap* **(David Martin)**
1982, Rourke Publications, Inc, USA
Hardcover edition of the first K9 book, published in Windermere, Florida, USA. No price listed. Back cover text is the same as the text on the inside front cover of the UK Sparrow Books paperback edition. This book has no series number or any reference to other titles in the series. The book's page proportions are the same as the UK edition with the covers being slightly larger than the pages. The interior artwork is identical to the UK edition; the text has been re-set in a larger font size. The Sparrow logo in the bottom corner of the front cover has been replaced with the Rourke logo.

BJU-004b *K9 and the Beasts of Vega* **(David Martin)**
1982, Rourke Publications, Inc, USA
Same basic description as above. Given the lack of a price on this and the previous listed item, these may have been library editions.
REF: ISBN 0-866-25115-4

BJU-003b

BOOKS, MEDIA STUDIES

BME-004a *Reading Between Designs: Visual Imagery and the Generation of Meaning in* **The Avengers, The Prisoner** *and* **Doctor Who (Piers D Britton and Simon J Barker)**
2003/06, University of Texas Press, USA
Media studies book which looks at the design of three television shows, one being *Doctor Who*. Softcover edition.
REF: ISBN 0-292-70927-7 OP: $24.95 p/b

BME-004b *Reading Between Designs: Visual Imagery and the Generation of Meaning in* **The Avengers, The Prisoner** *and* **Doctor Who (Piers D Britton and Simon J Barker)**
2003/06, University of Texas Press, USA
Hardcover edition. No dust jacket.
REF: ISBN 0-292-70926-9 OP: $60 h/b

BME-004a

BME-004b

FOREIGN DEVILS
Andrew Cartmel

BNO-004b

GHOST SHIP
Keith Topping

BNO-005b

BNO-006

BNO-007

BOOKS, NOVELLAS

BNO-004b *Ghost Ship* **(Keith Topping)**
2003/12/18, Telos Publishing Ltd, UK
Paperback release. Cover by Dariusz Jasiczak. Does not include the foreword.
REF: ISBN 1-903889-32-4 OP: £4.99 p/b

BNO-005b *Foreign Devils* **(Andrew Cartmel)**
2003/12/18, Telos Publishing Ltd, UK
Paperback release. Cover by Mike Collins. Does not include the foreword or the additional Hodgson story.
REF: ISBN 1-903889-33-2 OP: £4.99 p/b

BNO-006 *Rip Tide* **(Louise Cooper)**
2003/02/27, Telos Publishing Ltd, UK
Featuring the 8th Doctor. The deluxe edition is signed and numbered and limited to 800 copies, featuring an art plate by Fred Gambino. Foreword by Stephen Gallagher.
REF: ISBN 1-903889-12-X std; ISBN 1-903889-13-8 del
OP: £10 std h/b; £25 deluxe h/b

BNO-007 *Wonderland* **(Mark Chadbourn)**
2003/04/24, Telos Publishing Ltd, UK
Featuring the 2nd Doctor, Ben and Polly. The deluxe edition is signed and numbered and limited to 800 copies, featuring an art plate by Dominic Harman. Foreword by Graham Joyce.
REF: ISBN 1-903889-14-6 std; ISBN 1-903889-15-4 del
OP: £10 std h/b; £25 deluxe h/b

BNO-008 *Shell Shock* **(Simon A Forward)**
2003/06/19, Telos Publishing Ltd, UK
Featuring the 6th Doctor and Peri. The deluxe edition is signed and numbered and limited to 800 copies, featuring an art plate by Bob Covington. Foreword by Guy N Smith. The Deluxe Edition Novella was winner of the 2003 Balacron Designer Award.
REF: ISBN 1-903889-16-2 std; ISBN 1-903889-17-0 del
OP: £10 std h/b; £25 deluxe h/b

BNO-009 *The Cabinet of Light* **(Daniel O'Mahony)**
2003/07/10, Telos Publishing Ltd, UK
Featuring the Doctor. The deluxe edition is signed and numbered and limited to 800 copies, featuring an art plate by John Higgins. Foreword by Chaz Brenchley.
REF: ISBN 1-903889-18-9 std; ISBN 1-903889-19-7 del
OP: £10 std h/b; £25 deluxe h/b

BNO-010 *Fallen Gods* (Jonathan Blum and Kate Orman)
2003/09/25, Telos Publishing Ltd, UK
Featuring the 8th Doctor. The deluxe edition is signed and numbered and limited to 800 copies, featuring an art plate by Daryl Joyce. Foreword by Storm Constantine. This novella won the 2003 Aurealis Award for the best Australian Science Fiction novel, and was shortlisted for the 2003 Ditmar Award.
REF: ISBN 1-903889-20-0 std; ISBN 1-903889-21-9 del
OP: £10 std h/b; £25 deluxe h/b

BNO-011 *Frayed* (Tara Samms)
2003/11/20, Telos Publishing Ltd, UK
Featuring the 1st Doctor and Susan. The deluxe edition is signed and numbered and limited to 800 copies, featuring an art plate by Chris Moore. Foreword by Stephen Laws.
REF: ISBN 1-903889-22-7 std; ISBN 1-903889-23-5 del
OP: £10 std h/b; £25 deluxe h/b

BNO-012 *The Eye of the Tyger* (Paul McAuley)
2003/11/20, Telos Publishing Ltd, UK
Featuring the 8th Doctor. The deluxe edition is signed and numbered and limited to 800 copies, featuring an art plate by Jim Burns. Foreword by Neil Gaiman. The special edition was limited to 40 copies and came slipcased. This edition was the same as the deluxe edition, but featured three additional art plates (by Walter Howarth, Fred Gambino and Andrew Skilleter), an additional signature sheet signed by the three artists, and also a further additional signature sheet signed by Paul McGann.
REF: ISBN 1-903889-24-3 std; ISBN 1-903889-25-1 del; ISBN 1-903889-34-0 special
OP: £10 std h/b; £25 deluxe h/b; £80 special h/b

BNO-008   BNO-009

BNO-010   BNO-011

BNO-012 (with slipcase)

BNO-012   BNO-013

BOT-005 (standard)

BOT-005 (special)

BSC-015   **BSC-016**

CCH-021

BNO-013 *Companion Piece* (Mike Tucker and Robert Perry)
2003/12/18, Telos Publishing Ltd, UK
Featuring the 7th Doctor. The deluxe edition is signed and numbered and limited to 600 copies, featuring an art plate by Allan Bednar. Foreword by the Revd. Colin Midlane.
REF: ISBN 1-903889-26-X std; ISBN 1-903889-27- del
OP: £10 std h/b; £25 deluxe h/b

BOOKS, OTHER

BOT-005 *Doctor Omega* (Arnould Galopin, adapted and retold by Jean-Marc and Randy Lofficier)
2003/09, Black Coat Press, USA
Cover by Gil Formosa. Foreword by Terrance Dicks. A modern translation of a 1906 novel by French writer Arnould Galopin. The Lofficiers have basically turned a story which had a number of curious parallels with *Doctor Who* into a *Doctor Who* story in their retelling. Also available: Special collectors edition with the original Rapeno cover, which also features 22 original illustrations from the Galopin story by E Bouard.
REF: ISBN 0-9740711-0-2 std; 0-9740711-1-0 special
OP: $14.95 standard p/b; $19.95 special edition p/b

BOOKS, SCRIPT

BSC-015 *Doctor Who: The Audio Scripts* Vol. 2
2003/07, Big Finish Productions, UK
Four scripts from the Big Finish *Doctor Who* audio adventures. Cover by Paul Burley. Edited by Ian Farrington. Project editors: Gary Russell and Jacqueline Rayner. Managing editor: Jason Haigh-Ellery. Contains: *The Eye of the Scorpion* by Iain McLaughlin, *The One Doctor* by Gareth Roberts and Clayton Hickman, *Dust Breeding* by Mike Tucker and *Seasons of Fear* by Paul Cornell and Caroline Symcox. Also contains a selection of outlines and other material from the stories.
REF: ISBN 1-84435-049-5 OP: £15.99 h/b

BSC-016 *Doctor Who: The Audio Scripts* Vol. 3
2003/12, Big Finish Productions, UK
Four scripts from the Big Finish *Doctor Who* audio adventures. Cover by Paul Burley. Edited by Ian Farrington. Managing editor: Jason Haigh-Ellery. Contains: *Spare Parts* by Marc Platt, *The Spectre of Lanyon Moor* by Nick Pegg, *The Rapture* by Joseph Lidster and *The Chimes of Midnight* by Robert Shearman. Also contains a selection of outlines and other material from the stories.
REF: ISBN 1-84435-063-0 OP: £15.99 h/b

CLOTHING ETC., HATS

CCH-021 ABC Doctor Who Cap
2003, ABC, AUS
Black baseball cap with white *Doctor Who* TVM logo embroidered on the front.
OP: $22.95

CLOTHING ETC., KEY RINGS

CKE-023 Laser Etched Keyrings
2003, Product Enterprises Ltd, UK
Laser etched blocks on an illuminated keychain. Two designs: Dalek and TARDIS. Comes in a presentation box.
OP: £7.95 each

CKE-023

CLOTHING ETC., T-SHIRTS

CCT-105 'Destroy' T-Shirt
2003, ABC, AUS
Black T-Shirt with a design of a Cyberman with the words 'Destroy the Doctor' on the front. TVM logo. S/M/L/XL.
OP: $34.95

CCT-106 'Traveller' T-Shirt
2003, ABC, AUS
Black T-Shirt with a design of the TARDIS in the vortex on the front. TVM logo. S/M/L/XL.
OP: $34.95

CCT-105

CCT-106

COL-062

COLLECTIBLES

COL-061 Tardis Etched Cube
2003, Product Enterprises Ltd, UK
Laser etched block with a TARDIS inside. Comes in a presentation box. For the laser etched blocks there is also an illuminated stand available on which to display them (costing £9.99).
OP: £19.99

COL-062 Dalek Spacecraft Etched Cube
2003, Product Enterprises Ltd, UK
Laser etched block with the Dalek spacecraft from the second *Doctor Who* cinema film inside. Comes in a presentation box.
OP: £19.99

COL-063 Dalek Etched Cube
2003, Product Enterprises Ltd, UK
Laser etched block with a Dalek and the logo from the second *Doctor Who* cinema film inside. Comes in a presentation box.
OP: £19.99

COL-061

COL-063

HCR-044

HCR-045
(exclusive Stamp Centre design)

HOUSEHOLD ITEMS, CROCKERY

HCR-044 Dalek Film Mugs
2003/07, The Stamp Centre, UK
Four designs, all based on the *Doctor Who* films.
OP: £5.95 each

HCR-045 40th Anniversary Plates
2003/11, Cards Inc, UK
Four designs: *The Daleks, The Cybermen, Davros, The
Doctor*. The plates are limited to 2000 each, and each
comes boxed with a different numbered certificate of
authenticity. There is a fifth design, *The Doctor and Daleks*,
exclusive to the Stamp Centre and limited to 1000 units.
OP: £29.95 each   NM: £15

HCR-045 (four standard designs)

HOUSEHOLD ITEMS, GENERAL

HGE-037 Dalek Bottle Opener Key Chain
2003, The Stamp Centre, UK
A moulded metal half-Dalek which is also a bottle
opener.
OP: £12.50

HGE-038 Dalek Table Lighter
2003, The Stamp Centre, UK
Pewter lighter.
OP: £69.95

HGE-037 (front and back shown)

MAGAZINES, MARVEL

MAG-006b Doctor Who Magazine
2003 (every four weeks), Panini, UK
Panini's *Doctor Who* Magazine published every four
weeks. Issues released in 2003: 326-337 (12 issues).
Edited by Clayton Hickman. Assistant Editor: Conrad
Westmaas (326-329), Tom Spilsbury (330-337). See
next two pages for a complete cover gallery.
REF: ISSN 0957-9818 OP: £3.40 each

HGE-038

DOCTOR WHO MAGAZINE PREMIUMS

◆ ccasionally *Doctor Who Magazine* will include an 'extra' for readers. This list features those issues which came with a free gift or other notable give-away in 2003.

ISSUE/PREMIUM

326 Free Big Finish CD: *No Place Like Home*
337 Free Big Finish CD: *Living Legend*

#326

#327

DOCTOR WHO MAGAZINE COVERS: 2003 GALLERY

IN the second edition of the TOYBOX, we featured a comprehensive colour gallery of every *Doctor Who Magazine* cover since the beginning of the series. In this update, we present the

#326

#327

#328

#329

#330

#331

covers for all issues released in the 40th anniversary year (but only in black and white). The related specials can be seen in their own category on the following pages.

#332

#333

#334

#335

#336

#337

RADIO TIMES: DOCTOR WHO FEATURES/STORIES

ISSUE	COVER DATE	FEATURE/STORY
4158 (Vol. 319)	22 – 28 November, 2003	

Featured four alternative covers to celebrate *Doctor Who*'s 40th anniversary. Each featured a different Doctor in costume (or something approximating their costume): Tom Baker; Peter Davison; Colin Baker; and Sylvester McCoy. The covers could be placed together to form a single image. The issue also had a pull out souvenir magazine inside: *Radio Times Doctor Who 40th Anniversary Special*, edited by Anne Jowett.

RT #4158 (all four covers shown assembled into full image)

MAGAZINES, SPECIALS & ONE-SHOTS

MAS-002b *Doctor Who*
1975/76, Radio Times, NZ
A NZ edition of the *Radio Times* 10th anniversary special was included with the purchase of Levi's jeans at a men's clothing store (possibly the Hugh Wrights chain). Note the Levi's/TV2 sticker on the bottom corner.
OP: $1.40

MAS-002b

MAS-002c *Doctor Who*
2003/11, Radio Times, UK
Facsimile edition of the 10th anniversary *Radio Times*
Special. This edition has some alternative photographs
within it, and is printed on a thicker and better quality
paper than the first edition. However nowhere on it
does it say it is a facsimile nor does it state the actual
year of publication. The edition can be distinguished
from the original by looking at the title sequence photographs on pages 2 and 3. The original edition has
seven photographs from the second Pertwee title
sequence displayed, with each still repeated seven
times (and with the logo image once). The reissue has
a sequence of images from the titles, all of which are
different.
OP: £7.99

MAS-002c

MAS-041 *Doctor Who Magazine Special Edition
#4: The Complete Second Doctor*
2003/04/10, Panini, UK
A Special magazine containing facts and figures about
the Second Doctor. Cover dated 2003/06/04.
REF: ISSN 0963-1275 OP: £4.99

MAS-042 *Doctor Who Magazine Special Edition
#5: The Complete Eighth Doctor*
2003/07/10, Panini, UK
A Special magazine containing facts and figures about
the Eighth Doctor. Cover dated 2003/09/03.
REF: ISSN 0963-1275 OP: £4.99

MAS-043 *Doctor Who 1963–2003: We ♥ Doctor
Who*
2003/11/06, Panini, UK
DWM Special Edition #6. Celebrating the 40th
anniversary. Cover dated 2003/12/31.
REF: ISSN 0963-1275 OP: £4.99

MAS-041

MAS-042

MAS-043

SCA-024

SGC-011 (front and back shown)

SUNDRIES, CALENDARS

SCA-024 2004 Dalekmania Calendar
2003, Street Hassle Ltd, UK
2004 calendar. Design and text by Robert Fairclough.
REF: ISBN 1-843-38211-8 OP: £9.95

SUNDRIES, GREETINGS CARDS

SGC-011 Sylvester McCoy Xmas Card
1996, Just Postcards/Who Shop International, UK
Xmas card with a photo portrait of Sylvester McCoy in Season 26 costume as the Seventh Doctor. Inside the message reads 'Merry Christmas! Best wishes for 2095. Oops! Wrong time zone again'. The back of the card has the Who Shop International logo and their address.

SGC-012 BBC *Doctor Who* AudioCard
1998, BBC/Cartel International Ltd, UK
CD card featuring a recording of *Model Train Set* from BAT-005 read by Sophie Aldred. Card is mounted in a greetings card with an image of the TARDIS in the vortex and the TV movie logo. Text on front says 'BBC AudioCard - CD features a Dr Who story - Cards to listen to...'. Back of the card has the BBC logo and the Cartel International logo.

SGC-012

SUNDRIES, POSTAL ITEMS

SPI-033 *Doctor Who and the Daleks* **Movie Stamp Cover**
2003/07, The Stamp Centre, UK
Signed by Jennie Linden. Limited to 1500 covers.
OP: £14.95

SPI-034 *Daleks Invasion Earth* **Movie Stamp Cover**
2003/07, The Stamp Centre, UK
Signed by Bernard Cribbins. Limited to 1500 covers.
OP: £14.95

SPI-035 40th Anniversary Stamp Cover
2003/11, The Stamp Centre, UK
Signed by Tom Baker.
OP: £19.95

SUNDRIES, POSTCARDS

SPO-058 *Real Time* **Postcard**
2002/09, BBCi, UK
Postcard to promote the BBCi presentation of *Real Time*. Produced for the annual *Doctor Who* convention, PanoptiCon, held this year in Manchester. Artwork by Lee Sullivan, with print design by Kim Plowright.
OP: free

SPO-059 *Shada* **Postcards**
2003/04, BBCi, UK
Set of four postcards to promote the BBCi *Doctor Who* webcast of *Shada*. 4,000 were produced. Artwork by Lee Sullivan, with print design by Lee Binding.
OP: free

SPO-060 *Scream of the Shalka* **Postcards**
2003/11, BBCi, UK
Set of four postcards to promote the BBCi *Doctor Who* cartoon webcast, *Scream of the Shalka*. Print design by Lee Binding using Cosgrove Hall artwork.
OP: free

SPI-033

SPI-034

SPI-035

SPO-058

SPO-060 (one shown)

SPO-059

SUNDRIES, STANDEES

STA-005 Desktop Standees
2003/12, Cards Inc., UK
Designs: Tom Baker, TARDIS, Dalek, Cyberman,
Davros. Each standee is approximately 12 inches tall.
OP: £7.99 each

STA-005 (Cyberman and Tom Baker shown)

SUNDRIES, TRADING CARDS

Big Screen AE-3

STR-024 Big Screen Doctor Who
2003, Strictly Ink, UK
100 card base set. 12 Autograph cards. 14 Gold foil
Chase card set. 1 Binder exclusive Autograph Card
(Geoffrey Toone). See separate list for card details.
NOTE: Promo Card AE-3 was missed from the STR-
023 listing in the second edition of the *Toybox*:
AE-3   Trapped
OP: £15 base set

STR-025 Big Screen Binder
2003, Strictly Ink, UK
A special binder for the Big Screen cards. Came with
Binder exclusive Autograph Card (Geoffrey Toone).
OP: £19.99

STR-026 Doctor Who 1963-2003 40th
Anniversary Set Promos
2003, Strictly Ink, UK
10 card promo set:
PR1   Friendly Yeti?
PR2   Eighth Doctor & Grace
PR3   Davros make-up
PR4   DJ
PR5   The Doctor & Jo
PR6   Sea Devil
PR7   Drawing titles
PR8   Leela ready to go ...
PR9   Radiophonics
PR10   Coming beginning 2003 (title card)

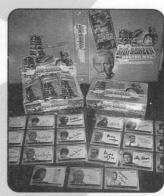

STR-024 (shown with binder STR-025)

Second 10 card promo set (produced for the San
Diego card fair/convention in July 2003):
B1   Title card   (NB; this is not the Brian
           Blessed binder card)
B2   Seventh Doctor
B3   Who's there?
B4   Daleks
B5   TARDIS
B6   Costume fitting
B7   Leela
B8   Yeti Unmasked
B9   Peri
B10   Movie

Also individual promos:
P1   Title card
CI-7   Peri
OP: £9.99 set

STR-025 (binder with exclusive card)

STR-027 (shown with binder STR-028)

STR-028 (binder with exclusive card)

Big Screen F1

STR-027 Doctor Who 1963-2003 40th Anniversary Set

2003/12/23, Strictly Ink, UK
100 card base set. 18 Autograph cards. 3 Costume redemption cards. 12 gold foil Chase card set. See separate list for card details.
OP: £15 basic set; £30 foils

STR-028 40th Anniversary Binder

2003, Strictly Ink, UK
A special binder for the 40th Anniversary Cards. Came with Binder Card B1, a Brian Blessed Autograph card.
OP: £19.99

STRICTLY INK–BIG SCREEN SET

THERE were 2999 wax packs made of this set. The prices are as stated in the Cards Inc customer catalogue *Ci Trader* May–July 2003. With regards to the quantities of the autograph cards in Strictly Ink's sets, they have said the following: 'there is never a set amount per person … [around] 4-600, sometimes only 100 cards for some people.'

NO.	CARD TITLE	
A0	Peter Cushing (Case Topper card). With facsimile signature.	

Hand Signed Autograph Cards

A1	Roberta Tovey	£35
A2	Jill Curzon	£35
A2	Jill Curzon Redemption Card: This is the standard, unsigned Curzon card with a yellow 'redemption' sticker on as she was delayed in signing the cards.	
A3	Bernard Cribbins	£25
A4	Ray Brooks	£20
A5	Keith Marsh	£10
A6	Philip Madoc	£10
A7	Geoffrey Cheshire	£10
A8	Jennie Linden	£20
A9	Barrie Ingham	£10
A10	Michael Coles	£10
A11	Yvonne Antrobus	£10
A12	Sheila Steafal	£10
A13	Binder Exclusive Autograph Card: Geoffrey Toone. Limited to 500 cards.	£20

Bonus Gold Foil Chase Set

F1	Movie Poster: Dr Who and the Daleks (Colour)	

Big Screen A0

Big Screen A13

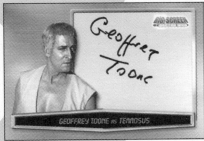

Big Screen F2

Big Screen 3

Big Screen 18

Big Screen 49

Big Screen 62

Big Screen 79

NO.	CARD TITLE
38	Destroy the Thals
39	Bridging the Gap
40	Do Not Move
41	Countdown Begins
42	Journey's End
43	Tug of War
44	Blasted Daleks
45	Control Attack
46	The Bomb Will Destroy the Planet
47	Firepower
48	My Lucky Number
49	Caped Crusader
50	Roman Reception

Daleks: Invasion Earth

NO.	CARD TITLE
51	Daleks Invasion Earth
52	PC Tom Campbell
53	Pull to Open
54	Time to Go
55	Louise and Susan
56	A Future in Ruins
57	Girders Collapse
58	Wyler Takes Louise
59	Grim Discovery
60	Saucer Over London
61	Quarry of the Robomen
62	Monster from the Deep
63	Resistance HQ
64	Saucer in Sloane Square
65	No Escape
66	You will be Robotised
67	Into the Compartments
68	The Resitance Attacks
69	Battle in the Corridors
70	Summoning Reinforcements
71	Hunting the Survivors
72	Battle Aftermath
73	Lunch with the Robomen
74	Bedfordshire Bound
75	Into Hiding
76	Dortmun's Sacrifice
77	Running the Gauntlet
78	Smashing Time
79	Saucer Attack
80	Tom and Louise Escape
81	The Mine
82	Cottage in the Woods
83	Sharp Practice
84	Betrayed
85	Grand Designs
86	Control Centre
87	Race Against Time
88	Overcooked Brockley

NO.	CARD TITLE
89	Reunion
90	Mine Ally
91	Roboman Rebellion
92	Ready to Fire
93	Bomb off Course
94	Magnetic Personalities
95	Black Dalek Down
96	Fleeing the Mine
97	Crash Dive
98	New Dawn
99	Bye Bye Inspector Campbell
100	Checklist

Big Screen 99

STRICTLY INK-40TH ANN. SET

THERE were 2999 wax packs made of this series. The prices are as stated in the Cards Inc customer catalogue *The Zone* Winter 2003. We understand that Tom Baker signed 500 copies of his card for the 40th anniversary set.

NO.	CARD TITLE	
Hand Signed Autograph Cards		
WA1	Eric Roberts	£75
WA2	Daphne Ashbrook	£55
WA3	Paul McGann	£55
WA4	Yee Jee Tso	£35
WA5	Sylvester McCoy	£55
WA6	Sophie Aldred	£35
WA7	Colin Baker	£55
WA8	Peter Davison	£55
WA9	Tom Baker	£65
WA10	Terry Molloy	£35
WA11	Peter Barkworth	£20
WA12	Tony Selby	£20
WA13	Martin Jarvis	£20
WA14	Sheila Hancock	£20
WA15	Elisabeth Sladen	£40
WA16	Sarah Sutton	£35
WA17	Richard Briers	£40
WA18	Burt Kwouk (Case Topper Card)	£55

Eric Roberts as The Master

40th Ann. WA1

Bonus Gold Foil Chase Set

F1	1977–Robots of Death/Weetabix cards
F2	1978–The Invasion of Time/Talking K9
F3	1979–City of Death/Candy Favourites
F4	1980–The Horns of Nimon/TARDIS Tin
F5	1981–K9 and Company/Viewmaster slides
F6	1982–Castrovalva/Easter Egg
F7	1983–The Five Doctors/ Doctor Who: A Celebration
F8	1984–Resurrection of the Daleks/Richard Hurndall

40th Ann. F7

40th Ann. CC2

Strictly Ink
40th Anniversary Set:
assorted autograph
and foil chase cards

Strictly Ink
40th Anniversary Set:
assorted regular cards

40th Ann. 17

NO.	CARD TITLE
F9	1985–Attack of the Cybermen/Doctor in Distress
F10	1986–The Ultimate Foe/Harry Sullivan's War
F11	1987–Delta and the Bannermen/Dalek and Cyberman plastic models
F12	1988–Silver Nemesis/Dapol toys
F13	1989–The Curse of Fenric/Script Book
F14	1996–Doctor Who: The Movie/Laserdisc

Costume Redemption Cards

CC1	Genuine Uniform as worn by Sgt Benton (John Levene)
CC2	Genuine Spacesuit as worn by the Fifth Doctor (Peter Davison) in 'Planet of Fire'
CC3	Genuine Army Uniform as worn in 'The Caves of Androzani'

1	Celebrating 40 Years
2	William Hartnell Remembered
3	Patrick Troughton Remembered
4	Jon Pertwee Remembered
5	Tom Baker Remembered
6	Peter Davison Remembered
7	Colin Baker Remembered
8	Sylvester McCoy Remembered
9	Paul McGann Remembered
10	Daleks Invade Hammersmith
11	Cybermen at St Paul's Cathedral
12	Daemons in Aldbourne Village
13	The Doctor in Portmeirion
14	The Doctor in Paris
15	Canal Route
16	On the Streets of Seville
17	On Location in a Quarry
18	Movie in Vancouver
19	The Power of the Daleks
20	The Krotons
21	The Macra Terror
22	The Moonbase
23	Inside the Spaceship
24	The Romans
25	The Dalek Invasion of Earth
26	The Web Planet
27	The Rescue
28	Planet of the Daleks
29	The Three Doctors
30	The Green Death
31	The Daemons
32	The Deadly Assassin
33	The Robots of Death
34	Destiny of the Daleks
35	Pyramids of Mars
36	City of Death

NO.	CARD TITLE
37	Earthshock
38	The Visitation
39	Castrovalva
40	The Twin Dilemma
41	Revelation of the Daleks
42	Attack of the Cybermen
43	The Greatest Show in the Galaxy
44	Silver Nemesis
45	Doctor Who The Movie
46	Writer – Terry Nation
47	Producer and Script Editor – Barry Letts & Terrance Dicks
48	Director – Christopher Barry
49	Set Designer – Roger Liminton
50	Costume Designer – Martin Baugh
51	Visual FX Designers – Mat Irvine and Tony Harding
52	Make-Up Artist – Dorka Nieradzik
53	Graphics Designer – Bernard Lodge
54	Composer – Peter Howell
55	Marco Polo
56	Galaxy Four
57	The Massacre of St Bartholomew's Eve
58	The Savages
59	The Tenth Planet 4 & The Power of the Daleks
60	The Highlanders
61	The Evil of the Daleks
62	Fury from the Deep
63	The Space Pirates
64	The Reign of Terror
65	The Crusade
66	The Daleks' Master Plan
67	The Celestial Toymaker
68	The Tomb of the Cybermen
69	The Ice Warriors
70	The Wheel in Space
71	The Ambassadors of Death
72	Frontier in Space
73	K-9 and Company 1
74	K-9 and Company 2
75	K-9 and Company 3
76	K-9 and Company 4
77	K-9 and Company 5
78	K-9 and Company 6
79	K-9 and Company 7
80	K-9 and Company 8
81	K-9 and Company 9
82	Erato
83	Early Cybermen
84	Evil of the Daleks
85	Diddy Dinos
86	The Beast
87	Vinyl Recordings

40th Ann. 26

40th Ann. 37

40th Ann. 63

40th Ann. 79

40th Ann. 95

NO.	CARD TITLE
88	Myrka Deaths
89	Wells Farrago
90	Double Take
91	Novelisations
92	VHS Videos
93	Records and Cassettes
94	CD Audio
95	DVD
96	Audio
97	New Adventures
98	New Media
99	Checklist 1
100	Checklist 2

TOYS, GENERAL

TYG-083j Chrome Gunner Dalek Rolykin
2003/11, Product Enterprises Ltd/Telos Publishing Ltd, UK
Limited to 600 units, this special chromed Gunner
Dalek Rolykin variant was commissioned by Telos
Publishing as a give-away with the second edition of
Howe's Transcendental Toybox.
OP: free with purchase of *Toybox*

TYG-084d Talking Daleks
2003/07, Product Enterprises Ltd, UK
New colours: Silver/black; Black/silver.
OP: £24.99 each

TYG-084e Talking Daleks
2003/12/31, Product Enterprises Ltd, UK
Special *Evil of the Daleks* edition for Alien
Entertainment in the USA. New colour: Silver/blue
with matt black dome.
OP: £24.99

TYG-083j

TYG-084d

TYG-084e

TYG-085b

TYG-085b Dalek Rollamatics
2003/07, Product Enterprises Ltd, UK
Four new packs released with the following new
colours: Gold/black, Black/gold; Grey/black, Black/white;
Red/silver, Gold/black; Silver/black, Silver/blue.
OP: £14.99 set

TYG-087b Remote Control Dalek
2003/07, Product Enterprises Ltd, UK
Red/black colour.
OP: £69.99

TYG-088 Inflatable Daleks
2003/09, Product Enterprises Ltd, UK
A 4 feet tall inflatable Movie Dalek. Limited to 3000
of each colour. Three colours: silver, black and red.
OP: £29.99 each

TYG-089 Talking Tom Baker Doll with Talking K9
2003/11, Product Enterprises Ltd, UK
Boxed set (box designed like police box with opening
front doors). Although main stocks of this did not arrive
until 2004, The Stamp Centre had some flown into the
country for the anniversary month, and they were on
sale at the Birmingham Memorabilia fair in November.
OP: £29.99

TYG-087b

TYG-088 (red version shown)

TYG-091 (closed and open)

TYG-089

TYG-090

TYG-090 Three Dalek Set

2003/11/20, Corgi Classics Ltd, UK
Boxed set of three Daleks: black/white, grey/black and
red/black. This set was exclusive to The Stamp
Centre. Limited to 7500 units.
REF: TY96204 OP: £17.99

TYG-091 TARDIS Gift Set

2003/11/20, Corgi Classics Ltd, UK
TARDIS design box containing: Gold/black Dalek, Bessie,
K9, Cyberleader and Davros. This set was exclusive to
The Stamp Centre and was limited to 5000 units and
came with a numbered authentication certificate.
REF: TY96205 OP: £31.99

TYG-092 Bessie and Doctor Who Models

2003/12/23, Corgi Classics Ltd, UK
Boxed set. Car has a small figure of the fourth Doctor
in it.
REF: TY96101 OP: £6.99

TYG-093 TARDIS and K9 Models

2003/12/23, Corgi Classics Ltd, UK
Boxed set. The TARDIS has a small figure of the
fourth Doctor in the doorway.
REF: TY96102 OP: £6.99

TYG-092

TYG-093

TYG-094

TYG-095

TYG-094 Dalek and Cyberman Models
2003/12/23, Corgi Classics Ltd, UK
Boxed set. Silver Dalek.
REF: TY96103 OP: £6.99

TYG-095 Doctor Who and Davros Models
2003/12/23, Corgi Classics Ltd, UK
Boxed set. Fourth Doctor figure.
REF: TY96104 OP: £6.99

TYG-096 Bessie, Doctor Who, Dalek and K9 Models
2003/12/23, Corgi Classics Ltd, UK
Boxed set. Silver Dalek. Fourth Doctor.
REF: TY96201 OP: £13.95

TYG-097 TARDIS, Davros, Doctor Who and Cyberman Models
2003/12/23, Corgi Classics Ltd, UK
Boxed set. Silver Dalek. Fourth Doctor. The TARDIS has a small figure of the fourth Doctor in the doorway.
REF: TY96202 OP: £13.95

TYG-096

TYG-097

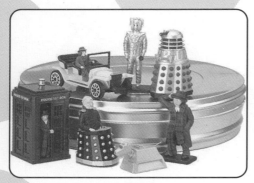

TYG-098

TYG-098 Film Canister Gift Set
2003/12/23, Corgi Classics Ltd, UK
Film can containing the set of Corgi models: TARDIS (with Fourth Doctor in doorway), Davros, The Fourth Doctor, Bessie, Cyberman, Silver Dalek.
REF: TY96203 OP: £27.95

VIDEO, BBC TV RELEASES

MANY of the Australian and New Zealand editions of the video releases were missed from the second edition of the *Toybox*.

VBT-010f *Terror of the Zygons*
2000/01/10, Roadshow Entertainment Ltd, AUS
REF: B00385

VBT-010g *Terror of the Zygons*
2000/01/20, Roadshow Entertainment Ltd, NZ
'PG' rating.
REF: Z00385 OP: $29.95

VBT-013f *The Daleks* **[Remastered]**
2001/04/02, Roadshow Entertainment Ltd, AUS
REF: B00407 OP: $31.95

VBT-013g *The Daleks* **[Remastered]**
2001/04/04, Roadshow Entertainment Ltd, NZ
'G' rating.
REF: Z00407 OP: $29.95

VBT-016f *An Unearthly Child*
2000/10/09, Roadshow Entertainment Ltd, AUS
REF: B00405 OP: $26.95

VBT-016g *An Unearthly Child*
2000/10/11, Roadshow Entertainment Ltd, NZ
'PG' rating.
REF: Z00405 OP: $29.95

VBT-099d *The Keys of Marinus*
1999/04, Roadshow Entertainment Ltd, AUS
REF: B00324 OP: $26.95

VBT-100c *The Face of Evil*
1999/05, Roadshow Entertainment Ltd, AUS
REF: B00325 OP: $26.95

VBT-100d *The Face of Evil*
2000/03/07, CBS/Fox, USA
REF: 2000026

VBT-102c *The Curse of Fatal Death*
1999/10/11, Roadshow Entertainment Ltd, AUS
REF: B00362 OP: $26.95

VBT-104d *The Greatest Show in the Galaxy*
1999/09/13, Roadshow Entertainment Ltd, AUS
REF: B00346 OP: $26.95

VBT-105c *The Invasion of Time*
2000/04/05, Roadshow Entertainment Ltd, NZ
'G' rating. Single tape.
REF: Z00396 OP: $39.95

VBT-106d *The Edge of Destruction* **and the Pilot Episode**
2000/05/08, Roadshow Entertainment Ltd, AUS
REF: B00404 OP: $26.95

VBT-106e *The Edge of Destruction* **and the Pilot Episode**
2000/05/10, Roadshow Entertainment Ltd, NZ
'PG' rating.
REF: Z00404 OP: $29.95

VBT-107b *Time-Flight*
2000/07/05, Roadshow Entertainment Ltd, NZ
'G' rating.
REF: Z00412 OP: $39.95

VBT-107c *Time-Flight*
2000/07/10, Roadshow Entertainment Ltd, AUS
REF: B00412 OP: $26.95

VBT-108d Cyberman Boxed Set
2000/11/01, Roadshow Entertainment Ltd, NZ
'M' rating. Embossed tin box set containing two
videotapes, *Attack of the Cybermen*(Z00449) and *The Tenth Planet* (Z00450) in separate plastic cases.
REF: Z00448 OP: $79.95

VBT-108e *The Tenth Planet*
2000/11/01, Roadshow Entertainment Ltd, NZ
'PG' rating. Withdrawn and recalled after it was discovered that the master used to produce the tapes did not contain the reconstructed fourth episode. Tapes were re-released in December 2000 or January 2001. 'Faulty' copies are in circulation.
REF: Z00450 OP: $29.95

VBT-108f *Attack of the Cybermen*
2000/11/01, Roadshow Entertainment Ltd, NZ
'M' rating.
REF: Z00449 OP: $29.95

VBT-108g *The Tenth Planet*
2000/11/13, Roadshow Entertainment Ltd, AUS
REF: B00450 OP: $26.95

VBT-110b *The Sun Makers*
2001/09/12, Roadshow Entertainment Ltd, NZ
'PG' rating.
REF: Z00515 OP: $29.95

VBT-111c *Four to Doomsday*
2001/11/05, Roadshow Entertainment Ltd, AUS
REF: B00519 OP: $26.95

VBT-111d *Four to Doomsday*
2001/11/07, Roadshow Entertainment Ltd, NZ
'PG' rating.
REF: Z00519 OP: $29.95

VBT-112b The Davros Collection
2002/04/01, Roadshow Entertainment Ltd, AUS
Card box set containing five tapes in individual plastic cases: *Genesis of the Daleks* (B00581); *Destiny of the Daleks* (B00582); *Resurrection of the Daleks* (B00088); *Revelation of the Daleks* (B00383); *Remembrance of the Daleks* (B00546). Limited Edition of 1000(?) copies, individually numbered.
REF: B00580 OP: $150.95

VBT-113b Master Boxed Set
2001/12, Roadshow Entertainment Ltd, NZ
'PG' rating. Embossed tin box set containing two videotapes, *Colony in Space* and *The Time Monster* in one double plastic case with a double-sided cover.
REF: B00539

VBT-113c Master Boxed set
2001/12/03, Roadshow Entertainment Ltd, AUS
REF: B00539 OP: $80.95

VBT-113c *Colony in Space*
2003/01/14, Warner Home Video, USA
REF: E1728 OP: $19.98

VBT-113d *The Time Monster*
2003/01/14, Warner Home Video, USA
REF: E1729 OP: $19.98

VBT-114b *Planet of Giants*
2002/03/04, Roadshow Entertainment Ltd, AUS
REF: B00569 OP: $31.95

VBT-114c *Planet of Giants*
2002/04/10, Roadshow Entertainment Ltd, NZ
'PG' rating.
REF: Z00569 OP: $29.95

VBT-114d *Planet of Giants*
2003/05/06, Warner Home Video, USA
REF: E1740 OP: $19.98

VBT-115b *Underworld*
2002/05/07, Roadshow Entertainment Ltd, NZ
'PG' rating.
REF: Z00578 OP: $29.95

VBT-115c *Underworld*
2002/05/13, Roadshow Entertainment Ltd, AUS
REF: B00598 OP: $31.95

VBT-115d *Underworld*
2003/05/06, Warner Home Video, USA
REF: E1741 OP: $19.98

VBT-116b *The Ambassadors of Death*
2002/07/01, Roadshow Entertainment Ltd, AUS
REF: B00621 OP: $31.95

VBT-116b

VBT-117c

VBT-118d

VBT-121d

VBT-116b *The Ambassadors of Death*
2003/10/07, Warner Home Video, USA
Also available as part of the 'End of the Universe' set
(VBT-125).
REF: E1856   OP: $19.98

VBT-116c *The Ambassadors of Death*
2002/07/02, Roadshow Entertainment Ltd, NZ
'M' rating.
REF: Z00621   OP: $29.95

VBT-117b *The Creature from the Pit*
2002/10/03, Roadshow Entertainment Ltd, NZ
'PG' rating.
REF: Z00599   OP: $29.95

VBT-117c *The Creature from the Pit*
2003/10/07, Warner Home Video, USA
Also available as part of the 'End of the Universe' set
(VBT-125).
REF: E1860   OP: $19.98

VBT-117d *The Creature from the Pit*
2002/10/08, Roadshow Entertainment Ltd, AUS
REF: B00599   OP: $31.95

VBT-118b *The Invisible Enemy*
2002/11/04, Roadshow Entertainment Ltd, AUS
REF: B00602   OP: $31.95

VBT-118c *The Invisible Enemy*
2002/11/05, Roadshow Entertainment Ltd, NZ
'PG' rating.
REF: Z00602   OP: $29.95

VBT-118d *The Invisible Enemy*
2003/10/07, Warner Home Video, USA
Also available as part of the 'End of the Universe' set
(VBT-125).
REF: E1859   OP: $19.98

VBT-119b The Time Lord Collection
2003/04/17, Roadshow Entertainment Ltd, NZ
'PG' rating. Card boxed set with three tapes in indi-
vidual plastic cases. Contains *The War Games*
(B00713); *The Three Doctors* (B00690) and *The Deadly
Assassin* (B00714). Limited Edition of 1000(?) copies,
individually numbered.
REF: B00683   OP: $99.99

VBT-119c The Time Lord Collection
2003/04/07, Roadshow Entertainment Ltd, AUS
Card boxed set with three tapes in individual plastic
cases. *The War Games* (B00713); *The Three Doctors*

(B00690); *The Deadly Assassin* (B00714)
REF: B00683 OP: $100.95

VBT-120b The First Doctor Box Set
2002/12/02, Roadshow Entertainment Ltd, AUS
Card boxed set with three tapes in individual plastic
cases. *The Gunfighters* (B00669); *The Sensorites*
(B00670); *The Time Meddler* (B00671).
REF: B00604 OP: $90.05

VBT-121a *The Mutants*
2003/02/17, BBC Worldwide Ltd, UK
Photo montage cover. 'PG' certificate. TVM logo.
REF: BBCV 7331 OP: £12.99

VBT-121b *The Mutants*
2003/05/05, Roadshow Entertainment Ltd, AUS
REF: B00715 OP: $31.95

VBT-121c *The Mutants*
2003/05/15, Roadshow Entertainment Ltd, NZ
'PG' rating.
REF: Z00715 OP: $29.99

VBT-121d *The Mutants*
2003/10/07, Warner Home Video, USA
Also available as part of the 'End of the Universe' set
(VBT-125).
REF: E1857 OP: $19.98

VBT-122a *Meglos*
2003/04/28, BBC Worldwide Ltd, UK
Photo montage cover. 'U' certificate. TVM logo.
REF: BBCV 7332 OP: £12.99

VBT-122b *Meglos*
2003/06/30, Roadshow Entertainment Ltd, AUS
REF: B00718 OP: $31.95

VBT-122c *Meglos*
2003/07/10, Roadshow Entertainment Ltd, NZ
'PG' rating.
REF: Z00718 OP: $29.99

VBT-122d *Meglos*
2003/10/07, Warner Home Video, USA
Also available as part of the 'End of the Universe' set
(VBT-125).
REF: E1862 OP: $19.98

VBT-123a *The Horns of Nimon*
2003/06/02, BBC Worldwide Ltd, UK
Photo montage cover. 'U' certificate. TVM logo.
REF: BBCV 7334 OP: £12.99

VBT-122a

VBT-122d

VBT-122a

VBT-123d

VBT-124a

VBT-124b

VBT-123b *The Horns of Nimon*
2003/09/01, Roadshow Entertainment Ltd, AUS
REF: B00731 OP: $31.95

VBT-123c *The Horns of Nimon*
2003/09/04, Roadshow Entertainment Ltd, NZ
'PG' rating.
REF: Z00731 OP: $29.99

VBT-123d *The Horns of Nimon*
2003/10/07, Warner Home Video, USA
Also available as part of the 'End of the Universe' set
(VBT-125).
REF: E1861 OP: $19.98

VBT-124a *Invasion of the Dinosaurs*
2003/09/08, BBC Worldwide Ltd, UK
REF: BBCV 7333 OP: £12.99

VBT-124b *Invasion of the Dinosaurs*
2003/10/07, Warner Home Video, USA
Also available as part of the 'End of the Universe' set
(VBT-125).
REF: E1858 OP: $19.98

VBT-125 The End of the Universe set
2003/10/07, Warner Home Video, USA
USA release of a boxed set of all the remaining *Doctor Who* videos yet to be released in the USA. Contains:
The Sensorites (E1852); *The Reign of Terror* (includes *The Faceless Ones* episodes 1 and 3, and *The Web of Fear* episode 1) (E1853); *The Time Meddler* (E1854); *The Gunfighters* (E1855); *The Ambassadors of Death* (E1856);

VBT-125

The Mutants (E1857); *Invasion of the Dinosaurs* (E1858); *The Invisible Enemy* (E1859); *The Creature From the Pit* (E1860); *The Horns of Nimon* (E1861); *Meglos* (E1862). The stories were also available individually.
REF: E1840 OP: $149.95

VBT-126a *The Sensorites*
2003/10/07, Warner Home Video, USA
Also available as part of the 'End of the Universe' set (VBT-125).
REF: E1852 OP: $19.98

VBT-127a *The Reign of Terror*
2003/10/07, Warner Home Video, USA
Also available as part of the 'End of the Universe' set (VBT-125). Includes *The Faceless Ones* episodes 1 and 3, and *The Web of Fear* episode 1.
REF: E1853 OP: $19.98

VBT-127b *The Reign of Terror*
2003/11/24, BBC Worldwide Ltd, UK
Boxed set containing the 4 existing episodes of *The Reign of Terror*, plus the remaining unreleased episodes: *The Faceless Ones* episodes 1 and 3, and *The Web of Fear* episode 1. Set came with a 40th anniversary pin badge. This is, for the moment, the final BBC release of episodes on video. The UK box set sold out very quickly and is now fetching upwards of double the retail price.
REF: BBCV 7335 OP: £19.99

VBT-126a

VBT-127a

VBT-127b

VBT-127b

VBT-127b

VBT-128a   **VBT-129a**

VDF-003d

VBT-127c *The Reign of Terror*

2003/12/04, Roadshow Entertainment Ltd, NZ
'PG' rating. One tape containing *The Reign of Terror*
episodes 1-3, 6 with linking narration by Carole Ann
Ford; *The Faceless Ones* episodes 1 and 3 and *The Web
of Fear* episode 1. Photomontage cover combines ele-
ments from the individual covers of the two individual
UK tape covers.
REF: Z00780 OP: $39.99

VBT-127d *The Reign of Terror*

2003/12/03, Roadshow Entertainment Ltd, AUS
REF: B00780 OP: $31.95

VBT-128a *The Time Meddler*

2003/10/07, Warner Home Video, USA
Also available as part of the 'End of the Universe' set
(VBT-125).
REF: E1854 OP: $19.98

VBT-129a *The Gunfighters*

2003/10/07, Warner Home Video, USA
Also available as part of the 'End of the Universe' set
(VBT-125).
REF: E1855 OP: $19.98

VIDEO, DVD FILMS

VDF-003d *Doctor Who and the Daleks...*

2001/05/24, Universal Pictures Ltd, NZ
'PG' rating. "35th Anniversary Collector's Edition", 1
disc, containing 2 feature films: *Doctor Who and the
Daleks* and *Daleks: Invasion Earth 2150 AD* plus
Dalekmania documentary.
REF: 0782342 OP: $39.95

VDF-003e *Dr. Who The Motion Pictures*

2003/02, Studio Canal +, UK
Gold edition boxed DVD set of the two cinema films.
Edition limited to 5000 units. Each contains the two
film DVDs as previously, and also contains two
'Senitypes' with an image from each film, and its cor-
responding 35mm film frame. Also contains two
reproduction campaign booklets, and two film posters
(as a mail in offer).
REF: G201354 OP: £44.99

VDF-003e

VIDEO, DVD INDEPENDENT DRAMAS

THESE are DVD editions of independent *Doctor Who*-related dramas.

VIV-001 *Mindgame*
2003/09/03, Reeltime Pictures Ltd, UK
DVD-R release of VID-010b.
REF: RTP0291 OP: £15.99

VIV-002 *Mindgame Trilogy*
2003/10/31, Reeltime Pictures Ltd, UK
DVD-R release of VID-011b.
REF: RTP0305 OP: £15.99

VDD-001   **VDD-002**

VIDEO, DVD INTERVIEWS

VDI-003 *Patrick Troughton in America*
2003/04/30, Reeltime Pictures Ltd, UK
Production looking at Troughton through the eyes of American fans and event organisers. Includes TV footage of his interviews. Also available on VHS (VOI-009) for £12.99.
REF: RTP0280 OP: £15.99

VDI-003

VIDEO, DVD MYTH MAKERS

THESE are DVD compilations of interview material previously released on video in Reeltime's *Myth Makers* series.

VDM-001 *Myth Makers: Graeme Harper and Nicola Bryant*
2003/04/30, Reeltime Pictures Ltd, UK
DVD-R release of the two interviews from VMM-049 and VMM-006. Includes new introductions by Nicholas Briggs and Keith Barnfather.
REF: RTP0282 OP: £15.99

VDM-001

VDM-002 *Myth Makers: William Hartnell and Jack Pitt*
2003/05/31, Reeltime Pictures Ltd, UK
DVD-R release of the two interviews from VMM-044 and VMM-046. Includes new introductions by Nicholas Briggs and Keith Barnfather.
REF: RTP0283 OP: £15.99

VDM-002

VDM-003

VDM-004

VDM-003 *Myth Makers: John Leeson and Mary Tamm*
2003/06/30, Reeltime Pictures Ltd, UK
DVD-R release of the two interviews from VMM-002 and VMM-022. Includes new introductions by Nicholas Briggs and Keith Barnfather.
REF: RTP0284 OP: £15.99

VDM-004 *Myth Makers: Sophie Aldred and Andrew Cartmel*
2003/07/31, Reeltime Pictures Ltd, UK
DVD-R release of the two interviews from VMM-019 and VMM-056. Includes new introductions by Nicholas Briggs and Keith Barnfather.
REF: RTP0285 OP: £15.99

VDM-005

VDM-006

VDM-005 *Myth Makers: Deborah Watling and Victor Pemberton*
2003/09/03, Reeltime Pictures Ltd, UK
DVD-R release of the two interviews from VMM-010 and VMM-011. Includes new introductions by Nicholas Briggs and Keith Barnfather.
REF: RTP0290 OP: £15.99

VDM-006 *Myth Makers: Ian Marter and Michael Wisher*
2003/11/30, Reeltime Pictures Ltd, UK
DVD-R release of the two interviews from VMM-012 and VMM-001. Includes new introductions by Nicholas Briggs and Keith Barnfather.
REF: RTP0294 OP: £15.99

VDM-007 *Myth Makers: Patrick Troughton and Shaun Sutton*
2003/12/31, Reeltime Pictures Ltd, UK
DVD-R release of the two interviews from VMM-054 and VMM-041. Includes new introductions by Nicholas Briggs and Keith Barnfather.
REF: RTP0295 OP: £15.99

VDM-007

VIDEO, DVD RELEASES

NOTE that the Australian and New Zealand DVD releases are identical.

VDV-001c *The Five Doctors*
2000/10/09, Roadshow Entertainment Ltd, AUS
'PG' rating. Simultaneous NZ release.
REF: B001989 OP: $34.99

VDV-003c *The Robots of Death*
2001/07/02, Roadshow Entertainment Ltd, AUS
'PG' rating. Simultaneous NZ release.
REF: B005049 OP: $34.99

VDV-001c

VDV-004c *Spearhead from Space*
2001/09/03, Roadshow Entertainment Ltd, AUS
'G' rating. Simultaneous NZ release.
REF: B005099 OP: $34.99

VDV-005c *Remembrance of the Daleks*
2002/05/13, Roadshow Entertainment Ltd, AUS
'PG' rating. The disc is mastered from the US NTSC
version but coded for Region 4, whilst the cover is
based on the UK Region 2 version. Simultaneous NZ
release.
REF: B005469 OP: $34.99

VDV-006c *The Caves of Androzani*
2002/01/07, Roadshow Entertainment Ltd, AUS
'PG' rating. Simultaneous NZ release.
REF: B005769 OP: $34.99

VDV-007b *Vengeance on Varos*
2002/01/07, Roadshow Entertainment Ltd, AUS
'PG' rating. Simultaneous NZ release.
REF: B005759 OP: $34.99

VDV-007c *Vengeance on Varos*
2003/03/04, Warner Home Video, USA
*Incorrectly listed in the second edition *Toybox*.
REF: E1718 OP: $24.95

VDV-008c *The Tomb of the Cybermen*
2002/04/01, Roadshow Entertainment Ltd, AUS
'PG' rating. Simultaneous NZ release.
REF: B005799 OP: $34.99

VDV-009c *The Ark in Space*
2002/06/03, Roadshow Entertainment Ltd, AUS
'G' rating. Simultaneous NZ release.
REF: B005779 OP: $34.99

VDV-003c

VDV-004c

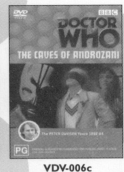

VDV-005c

VDV-006c

VDV-007b

VDV-007c

VDV-008c

VDV-009c

VDV-010b

VDV-010c

VDV-012b

VDV-012c

VDV-013b

VDV-013c

VDV-010b *Carnival of Monsters*
2002/09/02, Roadshow Entertainment Ltd, AUS
'G' rating. Simultaneous NZ release.
REF: B006099 OP: $34.99

VDV-010c *Carnival of Monsters*
2003/07/01, Warner Home Video, USA
REF: E1758 OP: $24.95

VDV-012b *The Aztecs*
2002/12/02, Roadshow Entertainment Ltd, AUS
'G' rating. Simultaneous NZ release.
REF: B006149 OP: $34.99

VDV-012c *The Aztecs*
2003/03/04, Warner Home Video, USA
REF: E1719 OP: $24.95

VDV-013b *Resurrection of the Daleks*
2003/07/01, Warner Home Video, USA
REF: E1759 OP: $24.95

VDV-013c *Resurrection of the Daleks*
2003/02/03, Roadshow Entertainment Ltd, AUS
'PG' rating. Packaged in a silver cardboard slipcase.
Simultaneous NZ release.
REF: B000889 OP: $34.99

VDV-014a *The Seeds of Death*
2003/02/17, BBC Worldwide Ltd, UK
Two DVDs. Extras on DVD: Commentary by Frazer
Hines, Wendy Padbury, Michael Ferguson and Terrance
Dicks; *Sssowing the Ssseedsss* documentary; *The Last
Dalek* 8mm home movie footage from *Evil of the
Daleks*; New Zealand Censor Clips; Photo Gallery;
Production subtitles; Tardis Cam.
REF: BBCDVD 1151 OP: £19.99

VDV-014b *The Seeds of Death*
2003/05/05, Roadshow Entertainment Ltd, AUS
'G' rating. Packaged in a silver cardboard slipcase.
Simultaneous NZ release.
REF: B006929 OP: $48.99

VDV-015a *The Talons of Weng-Chiang*
2003/04/28, BBC Worldwide Ltd, UK
Two DVDs. Extras on DVD: Commentary by Louise
Jameson, Philip Hinchcliffe, David Maloney, John Bennett
and Christopher Benjamin; *Whose Doctor Who* documentary; *Blue Peter* Theatre; Behind the scenes footage
from the making of the story; Philip Hinchcliffe interview from *Pebble Mill*; Trailers and continuity announce-
ments; Photo gallery; Production subtitles; Tardis Cam.
REF: BBCDVD 1152 OP: £19.99

VDV-015b *The Talons of Weng-Chiang*
2003/06/30, Roadshow Entertainment Ltd, AUS
'PG' rating. Packaged in a silver cardboard slipcase.
Simultaneous NZ release.
REF: B003519 OP: $48.99

VDV-015c *The Talons of Weng-Chiang*
2003/10/07, Warner Home Video, USA
Includes an additional feature: Howard Da Silva featurette. A 20-minute featurette that plays the Howard
Da Silva-voiced introductory narration for all 6 *Talons*
episodes used in the original 1978 US syndication
package by Time-Life Television. This time the producer has used the newly restored video from the DVD
and overlaid the narration on top of that, rather than
use the poorer quality 1978 broadcast masters as on
previous discs.
REF: E1814 OP: $34.95

VDV-016a *The Dalek Invasion of Earth*
2003/06/16, BBC Worldwide Ltd, UK
Two DVDs. Extras on DVD: Commentary by William
Russell, Carole Ann Ford, Richard Martin and Verity
Lambert OBE; CGI Effects; *Future Memories* documen-
tary; *Future Visions* documentary; *Talking Daleks* docu-
mentary; *Now and Then* locations visit; Script to
Screen; *Whatever Happened to Susan?* A BBC radio
play; Rehearsal film footage; Dalek Cakes on *Blue
Peter*; TV Trailers; Production Subtitles; Photo gallery.
REF: BBCDVD 1156 OP: £19.99

VDV-016b *The Dalek Invasion of Earth*
2003/08/13, Roadshow Entertainment Ltd, AUS
'PG' rating. Packaged in a silver cardboard slipcase.
Simultaneous NZ release.
REF: B007339 OP: $48.99

VDV-016c *The Dalek Invasion of Earth*
2003/10/07, Warner Home Video, USA
REF: E1813 OP: $34.95

VDV-014a

VDV-014b

VDV-015a

VDV-015b

VDV-015c

VDV-016a

VDV-016b

VDV-016c

VDV-017a

VDV-017b

VDV-018a

VDV-019a

VDV-017a *Earthshock*

2003/08/04, BBC Worldwide Ltd, UK
Extras on DVD: Commentary by Peter Davison, Janet
Fielding, Sarah Sutton and Matthew Waterhouse;
Putting the 'shock' into Earthshock documentary; CGI
Effects; uncut location film sequences; *Did You See?*
BBC review programme; Music only option;
Production subtitles; Photo gallery.
REF: BBCDVD 1153 OP: £19.99

VDV-017b *Earthshock*

2003/10/01, Roadshow Entertainment Ltd, AUS
'PG' rating. Packaged in a silver cardboard slipcase.
Simultaneous NZ release.
REF: B007349 OP: $34.99

VDV-018a *The Two Doctors*

2003/09/08, BBC Worldwide Ltd, UK
Two DVDs. Extras on DVD: Commentary by Colin
Baker, Nicola Bryant, Frazer Hines, Jacqueline Pearce
and Peter Moffatt; *A Fix with Sontarans* from *Jim'll Fix It*;
Behind the Sofa: Robert Holmes and Doctor Who docu-
mentary; *Beneath the Lights* documentary; *Beneath the
Sun* documentary; *Adventures in Time and Space* docu-
mentary; *Wavelength* radio programme; music only
option; Photo gallery.
REF: BBCDVD 1213 OP: £19.99

VDV-020 (exterior and interior box panels)

VDV-019a *The Curse of Fenric*
2003/10/06, BBC Worldwide Ltd, UK
Two DVDs. Extras on DVD: Commentary by Sylvester
McCoy, Sophie Aldred and Nicholas Parsons; Music only
option; Production Subtitles; Photo Gallery; *Nebula '90*
footage from a convention; *Take Two* BBC children's
show; *Modelling the Dead* documentary; *Claws and Effects*
documentary; Clean title sequences; a Special Edition of
the story with extra footage, new CGI effects and
remixed soundtrack; *Shattering the Chains* documentary;
Costume Design documentary; *Recutting the Runes* documentary on the special edition.
REF: BBCDVD 1154 OP: £19.99

**VDV-020 Doctor Who Dalek Collectors
Edition**
2003/10, W H Smith, UK
Limited edition of 5000 units exclusive to the W H
Smith chain. Boxed set of three Dalek DVDs: *The
Dalek Invasion of Earth*, *Resurrection of the Daleks* and
Remembrance of the Daleks.
REF: BBCDVD 1384 OP: £39.99

VDV-021a *The Three Doctors*
2003/11/12, Roadshow Entertainment Ltd, AUS
'PG' rating. The Australian release came out before
the UK release in this instance. Also released in NZ.
REF: B006909 OP: $34.99

VDV-021b *The Three Doctors* **Collectors Edition**
2003/11/12, Roadshow Entertainment Ltd, AUS
'PG' rating. Packaged in a silver slipcase with model
'Bessie'. The packaging is different to the UK release
of this edition. Also released in NZ.
REF: B007299 OP: $48.99

VDV-021c *The Three Doctors*
2003/11/24, BBC Worldwide Ltd, UK
Extras on DVD: Commentary by Katy Manning, Barry
Letts and Nicholas Courtney; *Pebble Mill at One* inter-
views; *Blue Peter* features; BSB Highlights; *Five Faces*
trailer; BBC1 trailer; Jon Pertwee, Katy Manning and
Nicholas Courtney on stage at a 1993 convention.
Photo Gallery and on-screen production notes.
REF: BBCDVD 1144 OP: £19.99

VDV-021d *The Three Doctors* **Collectors Edition**
2003/11/24, BBC Worldwide Ltd, UK
A limited number of the DVD came in a boxed set
which included a Corgi Bessie model.

VDV-021b

VDV-021a

VDV-021c

VDV-021d

VMM-057

VIDEO, MYTH MAKERS

VMM-057 *Myth Makers 56: Philip Segal*
2003/01/31, Reeltime Pictures Ltd, UK
Producer, 1996 TV Movie.
REF: RTP0260   OP: £12.99

VMM-058 *Myth Makers 57: Keff McCulloch*
2003/03/31, Reeltime Pictures Ltd, UK
Composer.
REF: RTP0261   OP: £12.99

VIDEO, OTHER INTERVIEWS

VOI-009 *Patrick Troughton in America*
2003/04/30, Reeltime Pictures Ltd, UK
Production looking at Troughton through the eyes of
American fans and event organisers. Includes TV
footage of his interviews. Also available on DVD-R
(VDI-003) for £15.99.
REF: RTP0263   OP: £12.99

VOI-010 *Colin & Katy Live!*
2001/08, New Zealand Doctor Who Fan Club, NZ
Recorded on 10 and 11 February 2001 in Auckland,
New Zealand. A video record of Colin Baker and Katy
Manning's on stage talks at the *Armageddon* 2001 convention, plus featuring an exclusive, private interview
with Colin Baker. Duration: approx. 2 hours. Approx.
30 copies produced.
REF: TSV Video 2   OP: $26.95

VMM-058

VOI-009

VOI-010

FROM THE WAREHOUSE

FOR these update editions to the TOYBOX book, we wanted to look in more depth at the companies and people who actually produce the *Doctor Who* merchandise that we love. We therefore contacted some of the people who had significant input into 2003's releases and asked them some questions about their ranges, their background and how they felt it was all going. Here are the results:

BIG FINISH

BIG Finish have been producing full cast *Doctor Who* on audio for several years, and recently branched out into publishing short story anthologies, script books and other book-based projects. The company is run by Jason Haigh-Ellery, and Gary Russell works for them on a freelance basis, arranging the primary *Doctor Who* audio line.

TOYBOX: *How, when and why did you decide to start producing* Doctor Who *merchandise? Was this an extension to existing ranges or was the company created to produce the* Doctor Who *items?*
Gary Russell: My involvement started because I went to Jason Haigh-Ellery for backing once Nick Briggs and I had secured the Bernice Summerfield licence from Virgin Publishing and Paul Cornell. Big Finish Ltd existed prior to that but hadn't done much so Jason suggested using it as the company behind the Benny stuff. As a result, our first couple of Benny releases were passed onto BBC Worldwide by Stephen Cole [then in charge of the BBC's *Doctor Who* releases] and they then asked us if we wanted to do *Doctor Who*.

What was your intention during 2003 with regards to Doctor Who *merchandise? Were you following any overall creative or business plan with regards to the releases?*
Because of the anniversary, we knew we were going to have to hit November with a biggie. But I also wanted to 'do a JNT' and have other celebratory things during the year – hence the two Doctors in *Project: Lazarus*, the three 'old villains' plays and a couple of experimental stories such as *The Pirates, Flip-Flop, Scherzo* and *Creatures of Beauty*. Alongside that, John Ainsworth got the *Unbound*s up and running which was an alternative take on the celebratory theme. I'm not really one for business plans other than acknowledging the need to put in one or two old monsters every now and again (which the villains trilogy delivered) and creatively, I just wanted the year to be memorable.

What considerations and restrictions, if any, were imposed by BBC Licensing on producing merchandise during the 40th anniversary year?
None whatsoever – with both the audio and books licence, they keep a close watch on what we do but are rarely anything short of obliging. The only hold up was over the use of the 40th anniversary logo which was conceived and approved too late for the first couple of plays we released in 2003.

Were there any ideas that were rejected outright either by yourselves or through discussion with BBC Licensing that you can talk about?

Nope. As yet, nothing has ever been vetoed outright other than a couple of cover images in earlier years. Experience has taught me what they do and don't like and as it's their licence, it's up to us to play the game and deliver goods of a look, quality and marketability they approve of.

What sort of process do you go through from conception to production to release on the Who *merchandise you produce? Does it vary in time, amount of work, etc., or is there a pretty stable process in place?*

It's become quite stable now, and I have a good relationship with the people who do the clearances both at BBCWW and other places such as Hancocks. Again, you just make sure you meet their criteria without sacrificing your own artistic criteria. Whether its the BBC, or anyone else in the world, working in licensed magazines over the years has taught me the worst thing you can do is argue with the licence holder and try to convince them you know their job better than they do. And if you do, you have to find a way to convince them it was all their idea in the first place. Of all the licence holders I've had to deal with, BBCWW are, honestly, the easiest and fairest.

Is there any one item that you are most proud of, something that epitomises what you're trying to accomplish as a Doctor Who *licensee? What has been your most successful item? Why do you think that is?*

Artistically? *Davros* excited me when I heard the finished play. Working so closely with everything, I rarely get the chance to be surprised or thrilled by a finished product these days, but this did it for me. I also love good covers and when Clay[ton Hickman] delivered the villains covers, or when Lee [Binding] gave me *Nekromanteia* and *The Pirates*, or indeed Steve [Johnson]'s cover for *Scherzo*, I was overjoyed.

What was your favourite Who *collectible from the past?*

From my childhood? It'd be a black Louis Marks Dalek. These days? It's either the Rollamatics or the Talking Daleks by Product Enterprise. And I love shiny DVDs.

What's your earliest memory of watching Doctor Who *on television?*
Episode 4 of "The Tenth Planet." For years I thought it was "The Savages," but when I saw an episode of *Timeslip* some years ago I realised my memory of seeing Chal peering through bushes was in fact Commander Traynor.

If you intend to continue to produce Doctor Who *merchandise, what sort of possibilities do you think the new series in 2005 will offer?*
Practically? More customers. Artistically? The chance to develop much of what we have established to a higher level.

What plans do you have for 2004?
Sleeping at some point and transferring my old VHS tapes to shiny DVD. Oh, you mean *Who*-wise? Ah, that'd be telling...

THE STAMP CENTRE

THE Stamp Centre in London's Strand has been producing a wide range of *Doctor Who* merchandise over the last few years, from their stamp covers to greetings cards, coasters and bottle tops. In 2002 they lost their licence from BBC Worldwide, but in 2003 managed to renegotiate it back again.

TOYBOX: *How, when and why did you decide to start producing* Doctor Who *Merchandise? Was this an extension to existing ranges or was the company created to produce the* Doctor Who *items?*
Steven Scott: The Dalek stamp in 1999 was the impetus. When we secured the licence having prepared our first cover, and realised that people liked what we had produced, it spurred us on to other ideas. There is a buzz that derives from being involved with a specialist collecting interest even if one is not a mega serious devotee oneself. I watched *Doctor Who* avidly as a child and to be involved with something for which I have such a nostalgic fondness is very satisfying.

What was your intention during 2003 with regards to Doctor Who *Merchandise? Were you following any overall creative or business plan with regards to the releases?*
The suspension of *Doctor Who* licences in 2003 meant that plans were shelved. It did provide the opportunity to explore the movie route to cater for the interest there. Many completists have enjoyed seeing the covers incorporating this angle and there is more to come.

What considerations and restrictions, if any, were imposed by BBC Licensing on producing merchandise during the 40th anniversary year?
See above, but at the 11th hour we resumed our licence so we did manage to squeeze a fortieth anniversary cover in.

Were there any ideas that were rejected outright either by yourselves or through discussion with BBC Licensing that you can talk about?
No.

What sort of process do you go through from conception to production to release on the Who merchandise you produce? Does it vary in time, amount of work, etc., or is there a pretty stable process in place?

Good question. The covers are the most difficult of the products that we create. There are so many different hurdles to jump with clearances etc., and we like to try and combine the launch with an open day. Turning the collectors centre into a *Doctor Who* emporium for a day is always a challenge.

Is there any one item that you are most proud of, something that epitomises what you're trying to accomplish as a Doctor Who *licensee? What has been your most successful item? Why do you think that is?*

The "Doctors United" cover was a colossal challenge. Liaising with seven different parties to bring it into existence took an immense amount of time. The "Assistants United" was not dissimilar, but for various reasons the satisfaction was not the same. These are items that the collectors really treasure and they have rapidly appreciated in price. The "Assistants" is actually the rarer cover. Only 500 were ever produced.

What was your favourite Who *collectible from the past?*

I may just have to treat myself to a *Doctor Who* pinball machine.

What's your earliest memory of watching Doctor Who *on television?*

Being petrified by the Cybermen. This was recently the source of one of the funniest incidents I have ever seen during our *Doctor Who* experiences (well, apart from when a Canadian visitor genuinely greeted Tom Baker as Mr Pertwee). A young child was brought to the event and was waiting in the queue when our visiting Cyberman emerged from our shop in all his very authentic glory. The poor boy was absolutely traumatised much to the amusement of everyone waiting which only served to make his ordeal and our mirth all the greater.

If you intend to continue to produce Doctor Who *merchandise, what sort of possibilities do you think the new series in 2005 will offer?*

I'm not a Time Lord, how would I know?

What plans do you have for 2004?

As we now have our licence back, the intention is to vastly expand what we have been doing. It would be great to be involved with the new series thereafter but we'll have to wait and see.

DOCTOR WHO MAGAZINE

▶ OCTOR WHO Magazine has been published regularly since 1979, and in 2002 celebrated 300 issues. The current editor is Clayton Hickman.

TOYBOX: *How, when and why did you decide to start producing* Doctor Who *Merchandise? Was this an extension to existing ranges or was the company created to produce the* Doctor Who *items?*
Clayton Hickman: It's all rather before my time, I'm afraid, as DWM is celebrating its 25th year of publication in 2004! Obviously things have changed hugely since the days of *Doctor Who* Weekly, not least as we are no longer published by Marvel Comics (and, indeed, are no longer 'monthly' but I guess 'Marvel Monthly' is still catchier than 'Panini Four-Weekly'), but we are still just a part of a successful portfolio of magazines published by our parent company – albeit one of the most profitable.

What was your intention during 2003 with regards to Doctor Who *Merchandise? Were you following any overall creative or business plan with regards to the releases?*
We had no major plans for 2003 aside from our usual commitment to 13 regular issues of DWM and three special editions. The only impact made by the anniversary was the decision to print a celebratory issue for November, plus to turn one of our special editions over to being a '40th Anniversary Special' as we couldn't bear the thought of breaking that glossy-special-every-ten-years chain! We did finally get our act together with regards to graphic novels of previous DWM comic strips, but though our licence from the BBC was granted in 2003, the timescales involved in such a project meant that the first graphic novel wouldn't see print until Spring 2004.

What considerations and restrictions, if any, were imposed by BBC Licensing on producing merchandise during the 40th anniversary year?
Nothing whatsoever. Indeed, our portfolio increased with the granting of a licence for graphic novels.

Were there any ideas that were rejected outright either by yourselves or through discussion with BBC Licensing that you can talk about?
We were asked by the BBC if we wanted to produce an official *Doctor Who* calendar for the anniversary year, but we declined as our workload was already quite large enough!

What sort of process do you go through from conception to production to release on the Who *merchandise you produce? Does it vary in time, amount of work, etc., or is there a pretty stable process in place?*
Obviously after so long in print, DWM is a fairly well-oiled machine, though recent innovations like the special editions and graphic novels often conspire to throw a spanner in the works. We have set deadlines, but breaking news stories often mean our deadlines get pushed back slightly, though we only have a short time in which to make last-minute changes before our 'window' at the printers will be missed – which cannot be allowed to happen.

Is there any one item that you are most proud of, something that epitomises what you're trying to accomplish as a Doctor Who *licensee? What has been your most successful item? Why do you think that is?*

It's very difficult to say. There are features and interviews that I'm very proud of across various issues, and I'm pleased that our range of special editions have been so favourably received. I'm extremely glad that our graphic novels are underway at long last – this being something that at least three previous editors have tried to get off the ground before me. I was very close to the DWM Anniversary Special, so there's a lot of me in there, and we tried a few tricks in that one which hadn't been tried before (our cut-out cover for example). But overall the thing I'm most proud of is that DWM is still here, quarter of a century on, and obviously still has enough appeal to make it a profitable concern despite the TV series upon which it is based having finished regular transmission 15 years ago. It's an amazing feat, and the prospect of a new series, and a new influx of readers, is extremely exciting. Actually, if you want just one thing I'm really proud of my involvement in, it's the comic strip (now celebrating 40 years of continuous publication), specifically the anniversary story "The Land of Happy Endings". All kudos to its writer Scott Gray, its artist Martin Geraghty and the painted colours from Daryl Joyce. Just beautiful.

What was your favourite Who *collectible from the past?*

I absolutely adored DWM as a kid, right from the moment I found it in my local newsagents at the start of 1986. I couldn't believe such a thing existed! It certainly helped to make me a fully-fledged fan during the 18-month hiatus. I also remember deriving enormous pleasure from the early video releases at around the same time, another thing which gave me the *Doctor Who* bug. But I think the thing I loved most of all (and I fear I may be the only one!) was the Build-Your-Own-TARDIS cut-out book from WH Allen. It might have been a bit rubbish, but the finished model was something I used to gaze at, enraptured, for hours on end. Explains a lot really...

What's your earliest memory of watching Doctor Who *on television?*

Odds and sods from the end of Season Eighteen really. Disconnected, hazy memories of the gardens of Traken and radio telescopes. I have no memory of the following season at all, but by Season Twenty I was watching regularly. I was even allowed to stay up late to watch *The Five Doctors*, which was terribly exciting!

If you intend to continue to produce Doctor Who *merchandise, what sort of possibilities do you think the new series in 2005 will offer?*

Lots and lots. We're still discussing the impact the new series will have on DWM, and there are lots of ways we can go. No firm decisions have yet been made, but I think we have to broaden the magazine's accessiblility to appeal to new viewers. We're extremely lucky in that we're working closely with Russell T Davies with regards to these changes, specifically to the DWM comic strip. So lots to look forward to, and plenty of room to expand the magazine's horizons. In the past, DWM never really took full advantage of its publication in tandem with an ongoing series, so this is something we have to get right this time around.

How have you found working on the Doctor Who brand? What sort of challenges are presented by having to work to a brand as defined by BBC Worldwide?

It's been a pleasure. The wonderful thing about DWM is that BBC Worldwide trust us to deliver the goods with minimal interference. They often use us if they need advice or information, so I think we're seen as unofficial advisers to the rest of their *Doctor Who* portfolio. It's possible things may change when the new series is up and running, but I think as long as we continue to justify Worldwide's faith in us, DWM will carry on for many years.

What plans do you have for 2004?

As I said above, we're in something of a state of flux as we work out the implications of the new series on the magazine, but otherwise things are continuing as normal. We have *The Complete First Doctor Special* being worked on at the moment, and that will be followed later in the year by a two-part special on Tom Baker's Doctor. The first graphic novel, "The Iron Legion," will be appearing in the spring, and we hope to have the second volume, "Dragon's Claw," out before the end of the year. In addition we're planning something special for October/November time, when not only do we celebrate 25 years of DWM, but we also reach our 350th issue. One way or another 2004 is going to be an exciting year for DWM, and I'm very glad to be a part of that.

BBC BOOKS

BBC Books took over publishing the *Doctor Who* novels in 1997, and since then have continued regular publication of them. The current consultant editor to the range is Justin Richards.

TOYBOX: *What was your intention during 2003 with regards to* Doctor Who *Merchandise? Were you following any overall creative or business plan with regards to the releases?*

Justin Richards: We were aware that there would be a lot more publicity in the anniversary year and made a conscious decision to produce an anniversary novel for November. That said, we decided it shouldn't be 'heavy' in terms of retreading old ground or including loads of flashbacks or whatever – and a typical 'Horror in English village' UNIT story with a twist seemed a good move. I was delighted that Terrance Dicks managed to persuade Barry Letts to work with him on *Deadly Reunion*.

Obviously the 'big book' was *The Legend* – which most of the fan-based reviews seem to have misunderstood the point of. The aim was to appeal to the fans, but to find a much wider audience of people who remember *Doctor Who* with affection. You couldn't produce a book that lavish and costly just for the 5,000 book-buying fans, it would have to retail at about £100. As it is, £40 for 400 pages is actually good value compared with other large format books. (Alan Titchmarsh's latest gardening book is £25 for 200 pages, for example, with far less illustration and only 4 colour process not 5.) Certainly the book hit the mark in terms of the sales figures, and it got excellent mainstream reviews in everything from Waterstones Magazine to *The Times*.

Were there any ideas that were rejected outright either by yourselves or through discussion with BBC Licensing that you can talk about?
We did consider doing a 'biography' of the Doctor, and that got as far as a worked proposal. Maybe in the future we'll come back to that, though possibly in a rather different form. We also planned at one point to include a DVD or a CD with *The Legend* but logistics and cost defeated us there.

What sort of process do you go through from conception to production to release on the Who *merchandise you produce? Does it vary in time, amount of work, etc., or is there a pretty stable process in place?*
The process for the novels is pretty standard. But as their schedule is set, the time we have depends very much on the author meeting their deadline. If they are late (as occasionally happens!) then everything else gets squeezed. It's a standard publishing process from proposal through drafts, edit, copy edit, proofing. We schedule roughly a year ahead always.

Is there any one item that you are most proud of, something that epitomises what you're trying to accomplish as a Doctor Who *licensee? What has been your most successful item? Why do you think that is?*
In the novels, I'm far enough removed now from the run of Eighth Doctor books from *The Burning* to *Escape Velocity* to look back and say: 'Yes, that was rather good and it achieved pretty much what I wanted.' Of the other stuff, I remain proud of the Script Book – as does everyone at BBCWW. But sadly, it demonstrates the point of the current fan-base just not providing enough of a market to do all the things we'd like. The Script Book was aimed at fans, not the general public. The result was that it didn't sell too well. It made a profit, it was worth doing, but it didn't do well enough to justify doing any more.

What was your favourite Who *collectible from the past?*
Tricky one, but I love the 1960s Dalek annuals – *The Dalek Book*, *The Dalek World*, *The Dalek Outer Space Book*.

What's your earliest memory of watching Doctor Who *on television?*

Daleks – probably from *The Dalek Invasion of Earth*, though it's from *Power of the Daleks* onwards that I really have strong memories of the programme.

If you intend to continue to produce Doctor Who *merchandise, what sort of possibilities do you think the new series in 2005 will offer?*
Watch this space.

How have you found working on the Doctor Who *brand? What sort of challenges are presented by having to work to a brand as defined by BBC Worldwide?*
The biggest challenges I find come out of working for and with a large organisation – BBCWW – for which *Doctor Who* is just a small part of their business, albeit one they regard with affection and respect. Combining that with working with authors who are, by their very nature, individual and for whom their current novel is their life can make for some interesting challenges!

What plans do you have for 2004?
Book-wise, 2004 is already over (I'm writing this in mid-January 2004, by the way). Well, we have to get the manuscripts in and edit them, but that's business as usual. The proposals are sorted, the catalogue text is already written, and the schedule is full. Roll on 2005.

TELOS PUBLISHING

TELOS Publishing were granted a licence to publish original hardback *Doctor Who* novellas in 2000, with the first title appearing in 2001. Along with David J Howe, Telos is run by Publishing Director Stephen James Walker.

TOYBOX: *How, when and why did you decide to start producing* Doctor Who *Merchandise? Was this an extension to existing ranges or was the company created to produce the* Doctor Who *items?*
Stephen James Walker: David J Howe and I have both been involved in the *Doctor Who* world for a very long time. Our first BBC licensed product was a 30th Anniversary calendar produced in 1992 for 1993, which we did with Mark Stammers under the name Vision Publications. In 2000, David approached BBC Worldwide to see if they would be willing to licence a new range of *Doctor Who* novellas. To his surprise and delight, they said yes straight away. One stipulation they made, though, was that they would deal only with a limited company, not with an individual. Consequently David set up Telos Publishing Ltd. I joined the company shortly afterwards, primarily to handle the business and financial management side of things, although I am heavily involved in the editorial and creative side as well. David had already used the name Telos Publishing once before, when he and Arnold T Blumberg had put out the first edition of *Howe's Transcendental Toybox*, and he had also acquired the Internet domain name www.telos.co.uk, so it seemed a good name for the company! We decided very early on that we wanted to publish other things in addition to the *Doctor Who* novellas, and in fact our first-ever book was the horror

anthology *Urban Gothic*, based on the TV series shown in the UK on Channel 5. We now have a good back catalogue of horror, dark fantasy, TV tie-in and classic crime titles, and are bringing more books out all the time.

What was your intention during 2003 with regards to Doctor Who *Merchandise? Were you following any overall creative or business plan with regards to the releases?*

We wanted to do two things. First, we wanted to bring out further titles in our *Doctor Who* Novellas range, at a slightly faster rate than we had done previously, and of course to make them as strong and as well-presented as possible. That was just a continuation of our usual schedule for the range. Secondly, we wanted to bring out a new edition of *The Television Companion,* specifically to coincide with the series' fortieth anniversary. The original edition, published by BBC Books in 1998, had been very well received, and a big success sales-wise, although for some reason, BBC Books had never distributed it to North America or anywhere else outside the UK. Then they wrote to us and told us that they intended to let it go out of print. The sales figures had fallen a little by that point, although by the standards of a relatively small publishing company like Telos, they were still very respectable indeed. Consequently we reclaimed the rights to the book, specifically with a view to publishing a new edition – revised and expanded – ourselves. I'm pleased to say that the new edition has been just as successful, if not more so, than the original.

What considerations and restrictions, if any, were imposed by BBC Licensing on producing merchandise during the 40th anniversary year?

There were no special restrictions imposed for the anniversary year. The only thing that BBC Licensing stipulated, as far as I can recall, was that the fortieth anniversary *Doctor Who* logo had to be used on the slipcase of the very limited special edition we produced for our anniversary title, *The Eye of the Tyger*. That special edition, which boasted not only the slipcase but also extra art plates and a Paul McGann autograph, was limited to forty copies – one copy for each year! – and cost £80 apiece. As we received far more than forty orders for it, names were drawn from a hat to decide who got a copy. We were happy to use the anniversary logo for that, and indeed would probably have wanted to do so even if the BBC hadn't asked us to.

Were there any ideas that were rejected outright either by yourselves or through discussion with BBC Licensing that you can talk about?

We did want to do a short story collection for 2003, but were told by BBC Licensing that BBC Books wished to keep that licence for themselves. Shortly afterwards, it was announced that Big Finish had secured the short story licence.

What sort of process do you go through from conception to production to release on the Who *merchandise you produce? Does it vary in time, amount of work, etc., or is there a pretty stable process in place?*

The *Doctor* Who novellas line has now completed, as BBC Worldwide declined to renew our licence, so no new titles are being commissioned. The way it worked, though, was that writers would send story synopses and sample text to us – sometimes 'on spec', sometimes because we had invited them to – and we would try to identify the strongest of these submissions for further development. When we found one we really liked, we would work with the writer to refine it and then, if all went well, commission him or her to write the full novella. This was subject to BBC Licensing approving the synopsis, but in fact they never turned down any of the ones that we submitted to them. Once the writer was under contract, David would then find an artist to produce the frontispiece for the book and – a bit later, once at least a first draft of the text was available – approach another writer to provide the foreword to the book. Later still, he would decide on the binding materials and so on to be used for the book. Again, this was subject to BBC Licensing's approval at every stage of the process. Even things that stayed the same from one title to the next – such as

the foil stamp of the *Doctor Who* logo on the cover of the book – had to be approved by BBC Licensing afresh each time. Eventually we would get the book typeset, and – once BBC Licensing had approved the proof – printed. Then it would go on sale. A truly huge amount of time and work was involved in producing each title in the range. Of course it did vary a bit – the editing process was a little more protracted on some titles than on others, for instance – but in every case it was a mammoth effort! We always devote a lot of time and energy to making Telos books as good as we possibly can – our motto is 'committed to quality'!

Is there any one item that you are most proud of, something that epitomises what you're trying to accomplish as a Doctor Who *licensee? What has been your most successful item? Why do you think that is?*

I think the novella that I am probably most proud to have been involved in publishing is *The Cabinet of Light* by Daniel O'Mahony, both because that is one of my personal favourites and because, although it wasn't planned that way, it also turned out to be the launch title for a whole new spin-off range for Telos, namely the *Time Hunter* range. The most successful of the novellas, sales-wise, has been the first one, Kim Newman's *Time and Relative*. The first title in any new range always tends to do exceptionally well, as a lot of people buy it to see what the range is like, or to have one example of it in their collection, but do not necessarily go on to buy the later titles. Of course, Kim also did a fantastic job on the story, as the very positive reviews, and the *Doctor Who Magazine* award, attest! I think our most successful *Doctor Who* item of all, though, is going to be the new edition of *The Television Companion*, certainly if sales to date are anything to go by – but of course we did not need a BBC licence to do a purely factual book like that; we did it as an unofficial and unauthorised guide.

What was your favourite Who *collectible from the past?*

I can't really single out a particular item, but I love all the vintage merchandise produced during the Dalekmania era of the mid 1960s. What appeals to me about it is not only the 'spacey' design look, which is so evocative of the period, but also the fact that these items were produced not as collectibles for fans – as virtually all of today's merchandise is – but simply as toys for kids to play with. Of course, that also has the downside that not that many copies have survived, and they can now fetch very high prices! I check out eBay every day, but some of the vintage stuff goes for far more than I can afford!

What's your earliest memory of watching Doctor Who *on television?*

I watched *Doctor Who* from the very first season. I was a young child when the series began, but certain incidents from *Inside the Spaceship* and *Marco Polo* always stuck in my mind, and I'm pretty sure I saw the first Dalek story, as I certainly knew what the Daleks were when they reappeared in *The Dalek Invasion of Earth*! I suspect I watched from the very first episode, as my dad liked TV science fiction, and I doubt he would have missed the start of a new series.

If you intend to continue to produce Doctor Who *merchandise, what sort of possibilities do you think the new series in 2005 will offer?*

I think there are a lot of possibilities. Telos already has firm plans for several further factual *Doctor Who* titles – not necessarily specifically related to the new series – and we will have to see what the future brings!

How have you found working on the Doctor Who *brand? What sort of challenges are presented by having to work to a brand as defined by BBC Worldwide?*

There are always challenges dealing with a licensed property like *Doctor Who*, and of course we were very disappointed not to get our licence renewed after the expiry of the initial term.

What plans do you have for 2004?

The last of the novellas, *The Dalek Factor*, was published in March. We are not permitted, under the licence agreement, to continue selling the novellas past the end of June, although we hope to be able to make arrangements for any copies still remaining at that time to be taken off our hands by a distributor or a dealer, so that the titles will remain available to buyers for some time after that, as long as stocks last. We will also be continuing with our *Time Hunter* spin-off range, and of course there is this update volume to *Howe's Transcendental Toybox*! As previously mentioned, we have a number of other things in the pipeline, but those probably won't start to appear until 2005.

2003 MARKET REPORT

FOR the first time, we asked a number of active *Doctor Who* merchandise dealers, retailers and collectors to offer their opinions on the state of the *Who* collectibles market and to report on sales activity in the anniversary year. Their contributions, presented here in their entirety, were based on, but not limited to, a questionnaire distributed to the participating parties by the TOYBOX. We must also stress that the observations and opinions expressed on the following pages do not necessarily reflect the views of the TOYBOX authors or Telos Publishing Ltd.

GENE SMITH

ALIEN ENTERTAINMENT

Alien Entertainment operates out of Chicago and is one of America's leading distributors of Doctor Who *merchandise. It is run by Gene Smith.*

TOYBOX: *What was the biggest/best seller in new* Who *merchandise for 2003? What was the slowest seller?*
Gene Smith: This has to be broken into a few categories:
Best Sellers
1. Big Finish - *Zagreus*
2. BBC DVD & Video
3. Prod. Ent. - Radio Controlled Daleks
4. Books - *Legend*
5. Misc. - 40th Anniversary BBC pin
6. Magazines - any of the Specials (try to find them today!)

Slowest sellers
1. Big Finish - Benny stuff
2. Desk standees (due to high cost)
3. Roll-A-Matics Daleks (now that they are discontinued they are selling better)
4. Books - *Dimensions in Time & Space*

Did the anniversary boost business at all or did things stay pretty much the same?
It helped quite a bit renewing interest in many categories. This may also be due in part to the announcement of a new series.

If you deal in old as well as new Who *merchandise, what differences if any do you see in those segments of the market? Was demand for the old up over demand for the new, or was it balanced? Any other observations about old vs. new products?*
The new stuff is always in demand as people want to keep up with the latest. Older products did quite well for us. Virgin & BBC books as well as back issue magazines are still

in demand as they are out-of-print. People who missed them or passed on them the first time are trying to catch up before the prices go up any more.

What was the most sought-after old piece (or pieces) of Who *merchandise in 2003?*
The 10th Anniversary special is one of the most asked for. We also sold quite a bit of the 25th Anniversary *Radio Times* Special.

If you do business globally, were there differences in the market from the UK to the US and other countries? Did prices fluctuate from one to the other?
Our business overseas has grown dramatically. This is due to several factors, including advertising and marketing on our part. But the declining US dollar has boosted our UK sales for back list Virgin books, and the fact that we still sell many of them at the original US cover price can't hurt.

Was demand higher in general from a particular geographic location, or did geography influence the specific items or kinds of items that customers were looking for?
We did a booming business on the US west coast as California was our best state to sell to. Illinois did well due to the fact that we have a retail store and the Chicago TARDIS convention. Internationally, the UK had our best sales followed by Australia then Canada. New Zealand was fourth.

How would you characterize the market for Doctor Who *merchandise overall in the 40th anniversary year?*
There was great selection and in many cases too much for most customers due to financial limitations. Some of the merchandise that was produced in small quantities or by companies who lost their licence will be going up in price in the not-too-distant future.

What are your general predictions for the market's performance in 2004 and beyond?
Steady sales to our regular customers but increases as we find new ones. The new show will help us even further.

Do you foresee a 'break-out' item or company that you expect to dominate the market in the coming year?
If you asked me that question two years ago, I would have said Product Enterprise, as they defined what can be done with *Doctor Who* toys and brought them into the 21st century. Big Finish was that company four years ago and they're still going strong today. I can't pick a company, but I think whomever gets the licence to the new show's merchandise will do extremely well. Let's hope the BBC remembers those who supported them in the lean years.

How do you think the new show will impact the Who *merchandise market?*
Things look good. With the series returning, many old fans will show it to their children and a whole new audience will be born.

Additional Comments/Observations:
A great seller for this year, for us anyway, will be our exclusive Talking Dalek. It will be the rarest one they have done, with only 1500 numbered units (they made 3000 of the white Imperial). I chose not to list that item above as it would not be proper and could be viewed as a plug.

MARK ROGERS

MALLARKEY

Mallarkey was set up by Mark Rogers to act as an online sales and wants forum for Doctor Who merchandise, and as a specialist alternative to eBay.

TOYBOX: *What was the biggest/best seller in new* Who *merchandise for 2003? What was the slowest seller?*

Mark Rogers: Mallarkey sellers specialise in hard to find and secondhand *Who* merchandise. That said, the Talking Dalek last year and the Remote Controlled Dalek this year have been big hits. The limited edition plates have done well.

Did the anniversary boost business at all or did things stay pretty much the same?
There has been a slow but marked increase in activity.

If you deal in old as well as new Who *merchandise, what differences if any do you see in those segments of the market? Was demand for the old up over demand for the new, or was it balanced? Any other observations about old vs. new products?*
As I mentioned, Mallarkey deals mainly in old and hard-to-find collectibles. These tend to be more sought after than the newly-published, for which people go to 10th Planet, or the Doctor Who Store, or Amazon.

What was the most sought-after old piece (or pieces) of Who *merchandise in 2003?*
Props always provoke a feeding frenzy on Mallarkey, as did a 1960s *Doctor Who* board game. In fact, all the board games do very well for us, the 1978 and 1991 one too. TARDIS keys do well. On the publication front, *DWB* back issues and *DWM* back issues go briskly.

If you do business globally, were there differences in the market from the UK to the US and other countries? Did prices fluctuate from one to the other?
Who only exists as a serious collecting pastime in the US, UK and Australia. Mallarkey is based mainly in the UK, where the majority of our stock is listed. US and Australian buyers are interested in pretty much the same things as everyone else!

Was demand higher in general from a particular geographic location, or did geography influence the specific items or kinds of items that customers were looking for?
No, there was no particular item.

How would you characterize the market for Doctor Who *merchandise overall in the 40th anniversary year?*
It is a buoyant market. Collectors are mainly interested in books and videos. Though everyone is looking for original props, when they become available, few can afford to buy them. In the run-up to the new series, there has not been much new merchandise issued, but what there is has gone very well.

What are your general predictions for the market's performance in 2004 and beyond?
We're looking forward to an enormous revival due to the new series.

Do you foresee a 'break-out' item or company that you expect to dominate the market in the coming year?
We anticipate that Product Enterprise will continue to do well with their high quality models. As the BBC licenses new books, videos and (we hope) merchandise, a new generation of collectors will be sucked into the market.

How do you think the new show will impact the Who *merchandise market?*
We feel that the new show will give the market a tremendous boost and we are looking forward to it like crazy ourselves.

Additional Comments/Observations:
We can't wait to see it!

KEITH BRADBURY
WHONA

WhoNA is run by Keith and Jany Bradbury and they supply Doctor Who *merchandise across North America.*

TOYBOX: *What was the biggest/best seller in new* Who *merchandise for 2003? What was the slowest seller?*
Keith Bradbury: WhoNA's biggest sellers included the following:
Big Finish's CD *Doctor Who: Zagreus*
"End of the Universe" VHS video box set
Dalek Tins (*Power & Evil of the Daleks*)
Marco Polo
Any *Doctor Who Magazine* with a free CD attached
All of the *Doctor Who Magazine* specials (8th Doctor special, etc)

Slowest (or most disappointing sellers):
Faction Paradox comic #2
The entire glass etchings line
Most anything that comes from The Stamp Centre (ink pens, first day covers, greeting cards, etc).

Did the anniversary boost business at all or did things stay pretty much the same?
The anniversary flooded the market, but sales were brisk. People ended up being a bit more selective in their purchases, but Big Finish CDs continued to fly off the shelf in spite of the fact that we ended up with about 6 new titles in the span of 30 days.

If you deal in old as well as new Who *merchandise, what differences if any do you see in those segments of the market? Was demand for the old up over demand for the new, or was it balanced? Any other observations about old vs. new products?*

Only CDs and videos sell well in the 'old material' line. Most other items drop off substantially.

What was the most sought-after old piece (or pieces) of Who *merchandise in 2003?*

Any of the old *Doctor Who Magazine* issues that had a free CD attached. Old charity anthology books had some demand as well.

If you do business globally, were there differences in the market from the UK to the US and other countries? Did prices fluctuate from one to the other?

Increase in exchange rates coupled with the loss of several US distributors made US prices go up substantially on some products.

Was demand higher in general from a particular geographic location, or did geography influence the specific items or kinds of items that customers were looking for?

Geographical tracking data not available, sorry.

In summing up, how would you characterize the market for Doctor Who *merchandise overall in the 40th anniversary year?*

Sales were up solidly in 2003, but perhaps not to the degree percentagewise with the abundance of new product on the market.

What are your general predictions for the market's performance in 2004 and beyond?

2004 will be strong.

Do you foresee a 'break-out' item or company that you expect to dominate the market in the coming year?

Breakout items: 8th Doctor CDs will continue to do well, as will the new DVD releases.

How do you think the new show will impact the Who *merchandise market?*

This depends on whether there is US distribution beyond BBC America (if even that).

ROGER SMITH
MR MODELS

Mr Models is a specialist model shop in Birmingham, England, run by Roger Smith.

TOYBOX: *What was the biggest/best seller in new* Who *merchandise for 2003? What was the slowest seller?*

Roger from Mr Models: First may I point out we are a models shop and only stock models and toys, so our range of *Doctor Who* is mostly toys. Biggest in what way? In units it would be the Talking Daleks. By the end of 2003, there were eight versions. New for 2003 were the black/silver and silver/black versions. Biggest in terms of money were the radio controlled Daleks. New for 2003 was the red version. The most sales for Talking Daleks were the black/silver version, but any Talking Dalek is always a good seller.

The slowest sellers were the Dalek roll-a-matics. You only got four new Daleks, one in each set. Also, the talking Toms, due to the fact they came so late – one week before Christmas – and had to be flown in. It was the same problem with the radio controlled Daleks the year before.

Did the anniversary boost business at all or did things stay pretty much the same?
Only a little in that any new Dalek will sell, plus more presents were bought for *Who* fans by non-fans.

If you deal in old as well as new Who *merchandise, what differences if any do you see in those segments of the market? Was demand for the old up over demand for the new, or was it balanced? Any other observations about old vs. new products?*
The old market is well up and Media Collectibles finishing [after losing their licence] helped sales. If sales had been that good to start with, they may still have been going.

If you do business globally, were there differences in the market from the UK to the US and other countries? Did prices fluctuate from one to the other?
Prices hold better abroad as there is less competition. It's very competitive in the UK, i.e. Talking Daleks are down to £20 plus free post in the UK.

Was demand higher in general from a particular geographic location, or did geography influence the specific items or kinds of items that customers were looking for?
Who is always big in the US and Canada, with Australia not far behind.

In summing up, how would you characterize the market for Doctor Who *merchandise overall in the 40th anniversary year?*
As always, Daleks sell.

What are your general predictions for the market's performance in 2004 and beyond?
The market will slow down. We're seeing the first signs now with the Clockwork Dalek slow, the Talking Tom slow compared to last year, and the Talking Davros cancelled.

Do you foresee a 'break-out' item or company that you expect to dominate the market in the coming year?
No. Product Enterprise is turning to Gerry Anderson toys. First signs say it will be bigger than *Who*.

How do you think the new show will impact the Who *merchandise market?*
It depends on if they get Daleks in. If there are new Daleks, yes [there will be an impact]; if not, maybe a slight impact. It depends if fans give it time and let it develop.

GEORGE MANN

OTTAKAR'S

Ottakar's are one of the UK's independent book chains and recently won the 2003 Bookseller of the Year Award. George Mann is a writer and acknowledged expert on the science fiction genre (including an Encyclopedia of Science Fiction from Gollancz, and a science fiction novella from Telos) and he runs one of Ottakars' flagship stores in the centre of Coventry.

TOYBOX: *What was the biggest/best seller in new* Who *merchandise for 2003? What was the slowest seller?*

George Mann: The Dalek audio tin. This did really, really well in my store, actually making it to the third bestselling audio book for the Xmas period. The reverse of that had to be *Doctor Who: The Legend* – too expensive and put together in such a way that it looked like it was trying to be a 'design' book, with too much gloss and not enough substance to warrant the price tag. The Big Finish CDs continued to sell well, the Eighth Doctor far better than the others.

Did the anniversary boost business at all or did things stay pretty much the same?

Yes, there was a certain uplift in sales but not hugely evident. As mentioned above, the official *Legend* book didn't do much, but the *TV Companion* did sell a lot, as well as the Dalek tin and the other BBC audios. We also shifted a fair few [Telos] novellas, although sales of these have seemed pretty consistent since. [BBC Books'] *Deadly Reunion* didn't fly out, certainly no more than any other *Who* novel from the BBC. These seem to be slowing down quite a bit. There was a time when I could shift about ten copies of each title in a given month; now that's down to about four or five. I put that down to all the silly arcs in the Eighth Doctor books that seem to have moved away too much from what the core readership want.

What was the most sought-after old piece (or pieces) of Who *merchandise in 2003?*

Not applicable, although we were asked for copies of the old 'Decades' books – *The Eighties, The Seventies,* etc.

Was demand higher in general from a particular geographic location, or did geography influence the specific items or kinds of items that customers were looking for?

I found demand for products much higher in my Walsall store than in my Coventry store, but I put that down to market forces. There are two other stockists in Coventry, at least for some of the product, a Waterstones and a Forbidden Planet. In Walsall I had a monopoly on the market. Across the Ottakar's group, demand fluctuates dramatically from town to town. It seems that demand (and thus sales) are higher in market towns like Walsall, Darlington, Slough and Sunderland than in the bigger urban centres such as Milton Keynes, Coventry etc.

In summing up, how would you characterize the market for Doctor Who *merchandise overall in the 40th anniversary year?*

Obviously I have a limited take on this as I only deal in books and audio CDs, but I thought there was a very mixed bag of product. The BBC audio product was excellent (ie: the Dalek tin), *Zagreus* was not (although it sold fairly well). The books were mixed too – *Deadly Reunion* didn't shift all that well, and neither did *Legend*, but the Telos books (particularly the *TV Companion*) did (spurred on by having signed stock, but we had signed *Legend* too). The Big Finish books didn't do much, even though the *Inside Story* is a half-decent read, mostly because they don't really know that much about book publishing and the production values on that particular book were so low, particularly when the price was so high. The earlier part of the year was mixed too; the Big Finish stuff ticked over well enough, the BBC books continued to decline, the Telos books continued to pick up, and the BBC audios were somewhere in between for much of the time.

What are your general predictions for the market's performance in 2004 and beyond?
I think the books will have to undergo a *radical* transformation if they want to claw back any sales. In light of the new TV series, I think they need to capture some of the new fans with books that slot in well with the series and drop the over-complex and generally alienating story arcs completely. The PDAs will continue to sell to the original fanbase but new fans will want *Buffy*-style tie-in novels that slot in between existing seasons and flesh out the gaps between episodes. I think Big Finish will continue to sell well, provided they don't alienate their fanbase in a similar way to the books by just doing whatever they like and driving things in too radical a new direction. I'm speaking from a purely marketing point of view, but people I speak to who listen to the CDs want a comfortable, traditional *Who* adventure from BF when they hand over their £13.99, not some radical departure (á la *Zagreus*), that, speaking to customers, seems to have put a great deal of people off the CDs completely. The BBC audios will carry on doing well, and I hope they will release more of the partially existing stories such as *The Ice Warriors* and *The Reign of Terror* as these are requested a lot. I'm not convinced the *Short Trips* books will remain commercially viable at their current price and format.

Do you foresee a 'break-out' item or company that you expect to dominate the market in the coming year?
Not now; Telos have ceased publishing *Who* books. I guess the BBC can get on with generating new product based around the new series.

How do you think the new show will impact the Who *merchandise market?*
Hopefully there will be a massive new fanbase created, with lots of the people who are into the US shows like *Stargate*, *Buffy* and *Smallville* getting into new *Who* and picking up tie-in product and books. I think there *might* be hard times ahead for Big Finish when all of the new merchandise hits the shelves, as people will be getting their regular fix from TV once again and will have a more diverse (and directly TV-related) range of products to spend their cash on

APPENDIX A: COMIC STRIPS

EIGHTH DOCTOR STRIPS

TITLE	ISSUES	ARTIST/INKER	WRITER
DOCTOR WHO MAGAZINE – published every four Thursdays by Panini UK Ltd. (09/96 –)			
Where Nobody Knows Your Name	239	Roger Langridge/ David A Roach	Scott Gray
Doctor Who and the Nightmare Game	330–332	Mike Collins/ David A Roach/ Dylan Teague	Gareth Roberts
The Power of Thoueris!	333	Adrian Salmon	Scott Gray
The Curious Tale of Spring-Heeled Jack	334–336	Anthony Williams/ David A Roach/ Adrian Salmon	Scott Gray
Doctor Who	337	Martin Geraghty/ Faz Choudhury(1-6)/ David A Roach(7)/ Daryl Joyce(1-6)/ Adrian Salmon(7)	Scott Gray
Bad Blood	338–	Martin Geraghty/ David A Roach/ Adrian Salmon	Scott Gray

APPENDIX B: UNRELEASED ITEMS

EVERY so often an item of merchandise is announced or advertised which, for various reasons, is then never released. The main volume features a much more extensive list of these items.

UNRELEASED/CANCELLED ITEMS

TITLE	YEAR	NOTES
Delta and the Bannermen	2001/06/13	Video to have been issued by Roadshow Entertainment Ltd, NZ. Scheduled but postponed and later cancelled due to rights issues. REF: Z00496 OP: NZ $29.95
City of Death	2003	Video to have been issued by Roadshow Entertainment Ltd, NZ. NZ release of UK 2001 reissue. First listed as 'pending' and later cancelled. REF: Z00562 OP: NZ $29.95

APPENDIX C: UNOFFICIAL/UNLICENSED ITEMS

WITH the continued popularity of online auction houses like eBay, there have been several instances of *Doctor Who* related items appearing for sale which are created specifically for the market. These include CD clocks, lighters, spoons and other crockery items with *Doctor Who* imagery on. There are also sales of original artwork, prints, scripts and other paraphernalia which are either fan produced items or which were never produced commercially. There have also been so-called 'production samples' of items which were never actually produced. While some of these might be genuine, where the items in question (like for example Dalek teapots) can literally be created one at a time on demand, it's hard to tell whether these are genuine 'production samples' or whether an enterprising individual is making them to demand. As always with eBay, the message is: let the buyer beware. Here are a few of the items we spotted over the course of the year on eBay.

UNOFFICIAL/UNLICENSED ITEMS

TITLE
Tom Baker caricature artwork
Daleks Tobacco Tin
Doctor Who Business card holder
Doctor Who Software Collection CD – 2003
Dalek Teapots

APPENDIX D: CORRECTIONS AND UPDATES

THIS volume of the TOYBOX primarily covers items released in 2003, but the main listing also includes some items which were missed from the main volume (copies of which are still available from Telos Publishing). In this section, you can find corrections and updates to the information in the main book. If there is anything in either that or this volume for which you can provide more information, then please write to us and let us know. Any such information will be included in future update volumes.

CORRECTIONS AND UPDATES

PG#	CODE	NAME or CATEGORY	NOTES
34	ADR-001e	*Doctor Who and the Pescatons*	Picture for this item is incorrectly captioned ADR-001d.
34	ADR-001f	*Doctor Who and the Pescatons*	Picture for this item is incorrectly captioned ADR-001e.
47	AOT-004	*Tardis* by Jack Mackrel EP	Misdated as May 1988 when it should be May 1998.
77		BOOKS, ANTHOLOGIES	"When the BBC took over the fiction licence in 1996…": should be 1997, not 1996.
83		BOOKS, BBC/8TH DOCTOR	"thus in May 1996 the last of Virgin's 'New Adventures' book was published…": should be May 1997, not 1996.
90	BBE-050	*Doctor Who: Grimm Reality*	The printing fault did not just occur in early review copies; many of these were sold through retailers (for instance Amazon UK's original stock of this title sent out to purchasers were the faulty printing).
95	BBP-024	*Doctor Who: Divided Loyalties*	Release date was 1999/10/04 (not 1999/07/05) and should therefore be coded BBP-026.
95	BBP-026	*Doctor Who: The Final Sanction*	Release date was 1999/07/05 (not 1999/10/04) and should therefore be coded BBP-024.
141		BOOKS, TARGET NOVELISATIONS	"*The Power of the Daleks* and *The Evil of the Daleks* appeared in 1992…": should be 1993, not 1992.
159	BTR-010g	*Doctor Who and the Abominable Snowmen*	Inside ISBN should be 0-426-10583-4 (not 0-426-01583-4).
171	BTR-022a	*Doctor Who and the Revenge of the Cybermen*	Missing '0' off front of ISBN.
183	BTR-036a	*Doctor Who and the Deadly Assassin*	This was not the last original hardback published under Allan Wingate: the following hardback, *The Talons of Weng-Chiang* (BTR-037a) was.
196	BTR-055f	*Doctor Who and the Stones of Blood*	Andrew Skilleter's name is misspelt 'Shilleter'.
210	BTR-082d	*Doctor Who – Mawdryn Undead*	This edition appears out of sequence; it should precede both BTR-082b and BTR-082c in the list as it is a January 1984 printing, and in addition has a lower price than either of the two other editions.
470	TYA-016j	'Boots' Dapol Dalek set	Original price was £9.99. Release date was around November.
559	VOI-007b	*An Afternoon with Tom Baker*	The coding of this item incorrectly indicates that it's a reissue of *A Sci-fi Audience with Tom Baker* (VOI-007a), when in fact it is an entirely different product.

ABOUT THE AUTHORS

DAVID J HOWE

DAVID has been involved with *Doctor Who* research and writing for over twenty years. He has been consultant to a large number of publishers and manufacturers for their *Doctor Who* lines, and is author or co-author of eighteen factual titles associated with the show. He also has one of the largest collections of *Doctor Who* merchandise in the world.

David was contributing editor to *Starburst* magazine and edited the book reviews column for that magazine for sixteen years. He is also reviews editor for *Shivers* magazine. In addition he has written articles, interviews and reviews for a wide number of publications including *Fear*, *Dreamwatch*, *Stage and Television Today*, *The Dark Side*, *Doctor Who Magazine*, *The Guardian*, *Infinity*, *Film Review*, *SFX* and *Sci-Fi Entertainment*.

He is on the committee of the British Fantasy Society and has edited their bi-monthly newsletter as well as editing and publishing several books for them, including the British and World Fantasy Award shortlisted *Manitou Man*, a limited edition hardback and paperback collection of short fiction by horror author Graham Masterton.

He wrote the book *Reflections: The Fantasy Art of Stephen Bradbury* for Dragon's World Publishers and has contributed short fiction to *Peeping Tom*, *Dark Asylum*, *Kimota*, *Decalog*, *Perfect Timing*, *Perfect Timing II*, *Missing Pieces and Dark Horizons.* and factual articles to *James Herbert: By Horror Haunted* (Hodder & Stoughton, ed. Stephen Jones). He wrote the screenplay for the 2004 DVD film release *Daemos Rising*.

ARNOLD T BLUMBERG

ARNOLD has been a *Doctor Who* fan since 1986. When he's not hunting for that elusive Pertwee annual, he serves as Editor of Gemstone Publishing, publishers of *The Overstreet Comic Book Price Guide* and *Hake's Price Guide to Character Toys*. He also co-authored *The Overstreet Comic Book Grading Guide*.

Arnold provides the internal layout and design for many of Telos Publishing's other books. He has also served as Senior Editor for *Cinescape Magazine*, and has written articles for *Overstreet's FAN*, *Comic Book Marketplace*, *EON*, *Dreamwatch*, and other periodicals.

He authored the online guide to sci-fi collecting in the "Sci-Fi-O-Rama" section of eBay, and has contributed short fiction to the *Doctor Who* charity anthologies, *Missing Pieces*, *The Cat Who Walked Through Time*, *Walking in Eternity*, and the forthcoming *The Cat Who Walked Through Time II*, for which he also read another contributor's tail (heh heh) for inclusion on a bonus audio CD.

He teaches courses in comic book literature, time travel novels, and web-based literature at the University of Maryland Baltimore County. He is currently pursuing a doctoral degree in Communications Design at the University of Baltimore, having already acquired a Masters in Publications Design from the same institution in 1996. You can find out the latest on all his projects at www.atbpublishing.com.